SHUNKA

Life with an Artic Wolf

Marika Lumi Morgan

J. N. TOWNSEND PUBLISHING
EXETER, NEW HAMPSHIRE
1996

Printed in the United States.

First published in hardcover as *Wolf . . . Kill!* by Van Nostrand Reinhold Ltd, Toronto, ©1976.

Cover photograph courtesy of Alar Kivilo.

Published by

J. N. Townsend Publishing
12 Greenleaf Drive
Exeter, New Hampshire 03833
603-778-9883
800-333-9883

ISBN 1-880158-09-4

LIBRARY OF CONGRESS CATALOGING-IN-PUBLICATION DATA
Morgan, Marika Lumi, 1943-
[Wolf . . . kill!]
Shunka: life with an Arctic wolf / Marika Lumi Morgan.
p. cm.
"First published in hardcover as Wolf ... kill! by Van Nostrand Reinhold,
Ltd., Toronto, c1976"--T.p. verso.
1. Wolves as pets. 2. Wolves--Biography. 3. Morgan, Marika Lumi, 1943-
. I. Title.
SF459.W63M67   1996
818'.5407--dc20   96-2430
                                                            CIP

Foreword

I t is gratifying to note that since Shunka's story was first published in 1976, wolves have been getting much better press, and there are now many champions of their cause. Where once David and I were hard-put to find a single memento with a wolf motif, wolf artifacts now proliferate in the form of calendars, T-shirts, mugs, jewelry and artwork. Wolves are making a comeback in Montana, Michigan, Wisconsin, and a few other states, and they are being reintroduced into Yellowstone Park, albeit under a cloud of controversy. This is all good news.

The downside of this newfound popularity, however, is the alarming boom in the wolf and wolf-dog hybrid pet business, which is not good news. Somehow, the wolf's image has made an improbable leap from "vicious killer" to gentle, loyal, family pet. Neither is correct, and the myth that wolves make perfect house pets can be just as damaging in the end as casting them as villains.

Wolves are wild animals with all the survival instincts of wild animals. They cannot be housebroken; they cannot be "trained" to respect your furniture, your favorite chair, or your rules. And they will constantly test you and challenge your authority. Raising a wild animal means having to adapt your living circumstances to the animal's unique needs. The alternative is to force him to adapt to your needs. The first requires a full-time commitment, endless patience, funds to build an appropriate compound, and willingness to leave your ego at the gate. The latter requires breaking the animal's spirit, which is cruel. In either case, most wolf owners find at some point they can no longer handle or afford their charges and the once-cute pet becomes an orphan all over again. Animal welfare agencies and places like Wolf Haven in Washington state, Colorado's Mission: Wolf, and Indiana's Wolf Park receive thousands of calls each year from wolf owners or wolf hybrid owners who can no longer handle their "pets." The proliferation of such refuges is a testament in itself that wolf ownership is a difficult proposition and generally not a good idea.

Another disturbing result of the growing popularity of wolves is the breeding and peddling of thousands of wolf hybrids, with often tragic consequences. Not only is the perception that wolf-dogs make good pets completely wrong, it is dangerous. Breeding a pure wolf with a domestic dog can produce a seemingly wonderful pet, but in reality, the offspring can be schizophrenic and unpredictable. I've heard that an Eskimo might let one of his sled dogs breed with a wolf to produce a strong, smart lead dog, but he won't turn his back on the animal.

Ironically, wolf-dogs are now being passed off as pure wolves, and as a result, the attacks on humans by these hybrids are blamed on wolves. Once again, in the end, the wolf is branded with an unearned and undeserved image as a vicious killer.

My hope is that Shunka's story will now serve a dual purpose—to further champion the cause of wolves, and to discourage anyone who might be considering adopting one from doing so. I would not trade my experience with Shunka, but I would not repeat it. It was beautiful, mystical, eye-opening, and gratifying. It was also difficult, frustrating, heartbreaking, and ultimately tragic.

The best way to love these magnificent animals is to honor their wildness and to work to preserve their habitats. It is also the greatest gift we can give ourselves and our children, because it is surely true, as Henry David Thoreau wrote, "in wildness is the preservation of the world."

Marika Lumi Morgan
Los Angeles, California
December, 1995

Preface

Wolf! A single word that triggers a variety of emotions and, depending on where you stand, conjures up myriad images. He is the ferocious, blood-thirsty beast who chased troikas, skulked menacingly in the forest, and ate little children for breakfast; or, the wolf is the gentle creature who nurtured Romulus and Remus and adopted abandoned children in India. He is also the brave and courageous hunter whose name was given to the strongest of warriors among the North American plains Indians. The myths and legends abound—stories that feed the imagination and further obscure the true nature of an animal once as common to the North American landscape as the buffalo and now faced with the threat of extinction. Only now are naturalists and environmentalists beginning to understand the complex nature of the animal and the vital role he plays in our ecological balance.

My story is that of one special wolf called Shunka who, for a while, shared our life and our home and gave us an invaluable insight into his world. Through Shunka we learned that the wolf—far from being the villain he is so often made out to be—is an affectionate, playful and shy creature.

It is impossible to love a wolf and not champion his cause. It was almost impossible for anyone to meet Shunka and not love him. In telling his story, it is my intention that more people get to know him as we knew him—perhaps it will help dispel some of the fears and prejudices so unjustly harbored against the wolf. Like every other living being, he too deserves his rightful place on this earth. There is a wisdom in nature's wildness that includes the survival of the wolf as a species—and his time is running out.

The experience of living and growing with Shunka was extraordinary, and I cherish it as a special time in my life. To write about it is to relive it again—the joy and happiness as well as the heartbreak and sorrow. I could not have done it without the person who brought Shunka into my life, David M. Ostriker. I am grateful for his patience and understanding and constant support which kept me going when I wanted to give up. I am also grateful for the encouragement given me by my editor, Garry Lovatt—because he believed in the story of a wolf. I wish to thank Alar Kivilo and Stephen Bower for their help with the photographs, and Mary Tribe for her constructive criticisms.

There are a number of other people who cannot go unmentioned—people who loved Shunka and became an integral part of his life, making each day a little bit happier. Our deep gratitude goes to David Coburn who, as director of the MacSkimming School in Ottawa, gave Shunka a new home and a rare opportunity to romp with hundreds of children and who, throughout, stood by him. I also wish to thank Helen Coburn for always making us feel welcome, and Neil Craig and all the staff at MacSkimming who championed Shunka from the very beginning. Most certainly, a special thank-you is due to friends like John "Shoney" Collins and Kathy Kennedy-Collins who took Shunka into their hearts and were always there to help at the most difficult times, and to Wendy Wank, who never tired of "wolf-sitting," as well as all the many other friends who cared.

Marika Lumi

"When a tame animal loves you, you are flattered; when a wild animal loves you, you are his slave."

Jack London

Chapter 1

How does a person raised in the heart of New York City end up playing father to a wild arctic wolf cub? As a boy, the only pet David ever had was a dime-store canary, and that relationship ended abruptly when his mother let the cageling fly out the window of their sixteenth-floor Manhattan apartment.

I sat and toyed with this thought as we waited in the cheerless, fluorescent-lit office of Toronto International Airport's freight terminal. I thought about the first time we had heard the eerie, lonesome howl of a wolf echo across the stillness of Algonquin Park. It had been like stealing a moment from another world, one that man had lost touch with long ago. For David, the wolf came to represent that lost oneness with nature. However, his passion for wolves began long before that night—before we left New York City.

The summer after we were married we camped across America. David had never before slept in a tent, cooked over a campfire or trekked through the backwoods wilderness. That summer he became an avid outdoorsman and passionate conservationist. Through the years I learned that nothing was ever halfway for David. Once something sparked his interest, he pursued the subject relentlessly until he exhausted all available sources of information. Our apartment soon overflowed with camping guides, wilderness survival books and wildlife studies.

Although his excessive enthusiasm had long ago exhausted my interest in the subject, I nevertheless glanced compulsively through wildlife and nature sections in bookstores. One day I happened on a little book telling a remarkable story of a family of arctic wolves fighting for survival in Canada's inhospitable North. The book marked the beginning of David's love affair with *Canis lupus*. Wolves became his favorite topic of conversation, and he talked and read about them endlessly. He tracked down out-of-print texts on wolves and dropped in on pet shops in the hope of finding an abandoned cub. I shuddered at the thought of a wolf romping through our small third floor walk-up apartment, already crowded with six cats.

Fortunately I didn't have to worry too much about a wolf moving in with us, because we were moving out. Not only had our apartment become too crowded, as far as we were concerned New York City had become too crowded. We packed our bags, cats, and wolf books, and headed for Toronto.

Unlike the United States, where wolves are nearing extinction, Canada still has a relatively healthy lupine population, particularly in areas like Algonquin Park where they are protected by law. The odds for coming up with a wolf cub in Canada were good, and David intensified his search. He asked hunters and trappers in the north to keep an eye open for a motherless cub; he wrote to game farms, visited zoos and pet shops. I didn't give his project much thought. Eventually, I figured, he would exhaust the subject, or it would exhaust him. I never believed it would happen—but when it did, I forgot my reluctance and was as excited and happy as David.

I glanced at the clock. Almost two hours had passed since the flight from Edmonton had arrived. Perhaps something had gone wrong. David again approached the front desk. "Any word?" he asked the clerk behind the counter.

"Nope," the man answered without looking up from his newspaper.

"Maybe we should check with your people on the other end—just to make sure he was put on the flight," David persisted.

The man glanced at him. "I wouldn't worry about it. You've got your waybill number. I'm sure he's on the plane."

A few more minutes passed. "It's really pouring out," I said, glancing apprehensively out the window. "Maybe he's getting soaked, sitting alone on a runway somewhere—scared to death."

"There is nothing we can do about it, so you may as well stop worrying." David's voice was tense with anger, and I knew enough to keep my mouth shut.

One more tedious hour passed. A woman arrived to pick up her cat and became hysterical when the animal could not be located. We wondered if the same fate awaited us. A man came in to pick up two leopards for a zoo up north—and gave us a quick rundown on what to feed wolves. For the rest of the night, the freight office remained empty and silent. It was almost midnight when the clerk announced our cargo had been off-loaded. "You want to sign these papers?" he asked, indicating a line marked with an X. "Also, that'll be another $19.25 for the kennel. Forgot to charge you for it earlier."

We quickly completed the paperwork, and, while David was getting the car, I examined the official document which read "PERMIT TO EXPORT ... ONE LIVE WOLF." After all the waiting, it now seemed somewhat unreal, and I wondered what we had gotten ourselves into.

The freight depot was a cavernous warehouse piled with endless rows of boxes, crates and trunks. The Land Rover was already backed up to the loading dock and David had given our waybill to the attendant on duty. Moments later the man appeared wheeling a dolly loaded with a wire cage. He dumped it in front of us. "Here he is," he said. "He's all yours."

I leaned down and looked at the furry little creature that would come to dominate our household and our lives for the next year. He sat huddled in a corner of the cage, quiet, dazed and trembling. As

David fumbled with the lock, I timidly poked a finger through the wires and scratched a furry flank pressed against the side of the cage. Another freight employee appeared, and the two men stood around gaping at the cub. "What're you going to do with a wolf?" one of them asked. "Sell it to a zoo?"

"Nope," David answered, "we're keeping him."

"Oh, going to use him for breeding, eh?"

"Nope. Just keeping him." David was getting impatient with the lock. "Can you give me a hand with this?" he asked one of the men.

The man he had addressed stepped a little closer and then stopped. Pointing toward the cage he said, "Lift that little latch and slide it to the left." He then returned to his observation post and continued to stare while David fiddled some more with the lock. Finally, the door swung open. Slowly David reached into the cage and slipped a collar and leash around Shunka's neck. It was an unnecessary gesture. Shunka made no move to escape. In fact, he made no move at all. David gently lifted the limp body out of the cage. As if grateful for the security of strong, loving arms, Shunka sighed deeply and leaned against David, who looked at me and smiled sheepishly.

Driving back to the city I listened to David speak softly to the wolf cub nestled in his arms. I was surprised how fast Shunka had grown. He had become long-legged and gangly, and his head appeared too big for his body. It was now mid-August, and I guessed he was approximately eight weeks old. The last time we had seen him was early in July, when he had been a four-week-old ball of fluff. It didn't seem that long ago. We had been camping again, traveling west through Canada, three of us crammed into the small but sturdy Land Rover— David, my sixteen-year-old brother Sven, and I. Rain had followed us all through Saskatchewan and into northern Alberta, and we were damp and dispirited when David pulled into a campsite near the Alberta Game Farm. He had insisted on this detour. He was still in search of a wolf cub, and the odds were good the Game Farm would have one.

The following morning, bright sunlight crept into the tent, and we welcomed it as a good omen. Spirits were high as we piled into the

Land Rover and headed for the farm.

The first pens we encountered were the wolf pens—a series of interconnecting enclosures, spacious and heavily treed. A pack of twenty or more wolves wandered around the compound, and we watched them for a long time, marveling at their beauty and grace. One almost never sees a wolf in the wilderness—he is one of nature's wildest and shyest creatures, and he is terrified of man. These animals, however, seemed oblivious of the crowds passing by their pens, and it was a pleasure to watch them as they calmly went about their business.

Eventually, we observed a definite pack structure among these captive wolves. The dominant, or "alpha" male, was a magnificent gray timber wolf, lean and powerful. On several occasions, other wolves approached him with attitudes indicating inferiority. Some rolled over on their backs in a demonstration of complete submission; others crouched in front of him, tails low, ears back and close to the head, their tongues quickly and repeatedly licking the big gray's nose.

The wolf exists within a highly organized society, and a pecking order extends throughout an entire pack. Each wolf is aware of his position in the hierarchy and behaves appropriately towards all other members of the pack. As a result of this complex communication system, social harmony is maintained with little or no fighting within the pack.

As we stood by the pens, other people stopped to stare at the wolves, and we were surprised by their comments. "Amazing how much they look like dogs—and yet they'll tear you to pieces," one father said to his son. The most common remark seemed to be, "Vicious animals—you can tell by their evil eyes."

The wolf is probably the most misunderstood of animals—hated and feared because he kills to live, and his eerie howl can make your hair stand on end. The Big Bad Wolf image created by stories such as "Little Red Riding Hood" and "The Three Little Pigs" has helped create a deep-seated negative image of these predators—in spite of all the evidence pointing to the fact that wolves do not impersonate grandmothers or blow houses down. Nor do normal, healthy wolves attack people. There is no authenticated case in North America of a healthy wolf attacking a human being. Nevertheless, the frightening tales persist, and the wolf has been branded a murderous outlaw.

Sven and I finally left David at the wolf compound and continued our tour of the one-thousand-acre farm. Many hours and boxes of popcorn later, we were wearily contemplating the buffalo herd when David came running toward us, madly waving his arms, his face flushed. "I've found the cubs!" he shouted, and back we went to the wolf pens.

A short distance from the main compound, we peered into a small wire cage and counted four balls of beige fluff. I'm not sure what I had expected, but these little creatures resembled woolly wind-up toys rather than wild arctic wolves. Their faces were round, with pug noses and small floppy ears. Their tails were short and mousy; and fat, rotund bellies dragged along the ground as the cubs wobbled around on short, unsteady legs. "So these represent the Great Terrors of the North," I thought, watching them romp and wrestle with each other, squealing and yelping as needle-sharp teeth latched onto tails and ears.

The playful wrestling stopped abruptly and turned into a ferocious battle when a woman appeared with a tray of milk and Pablum which she set before the cubs. Wolves take eating very seriously, and these cubs were already aware that a dominant wolf is a well-fed wolf. It was an amusing sight as these mini-predators growled and snapped over their Pablum, but in the wild a wolf's ability to establish his status within the pack could mean his survival.

In an organized pack, the alpha male and female eat first while all other pack members sit back and wait. Not until these two have finished gorging themselves are the others permitted to eat—at which point dinner becomes a mad free-for-all accompanied by tearing, growling and snapping. If the kill happens to be small, the bottom wolf on the totem pole often ends up with little more than a well-gnawed bone to appease his hunger. But such is nature's law—survival of the fittest. If the pack is to survive to hunt again, its strongest and best wolves must survive.

Now that we had found the cubs, our next problem was to find

Al Oeming, owner of the Game Farm. Al had taken off on his rounds. He was a man constantly on the move, and by the time we flagged down his green pickup, the afternoon shadows were long and most of the tourists had left for the day. Word had apparently reached him that we were interested in the wolves. He cheerfully waved at us, shouted that we should go in and play with the cubs—and then took off to feed his giraffes the twigs and branches piled high in the back of his truck.

At a loss as to how we were going to get in the pen to "play with the cubs," David, Sven and I returned to the wolf compound and prepared to wait. A small sign identified the pups as Mackenzie Valley wolves. (North American wolves are generally divided into two groups—the commonly known gray timber wolf who inhabits the forested areas; and the shaggier, larger arctic wolf, usually biege or white in color, who roams the tundra. A designation such as "Mackenzie Valley wolf" is a fine-line regional distinction.)

"Perfect," I said to David. "Arctic wolf pups, just like the ones in *Never Cry Wolf.*"

In less than a minute, a young boy appeared carrying a large ring of keys. Al's communication system was mysteriously efficient. "Al said I should let you in to play with the cubs," he said and began unfastening a series of locks and chains. The wolves were three or four weeks old, he explained, and they were orphans. "Indian trapper dug them out of their den and brought them in a couple of weeks ago. Hunters killed off the mother." Our dismay at this chilling information turned to delight as we entered the pen and were greeted by an onslaught of furry bodies which clung to pants, wriggled between legs and squirmed to be picked up. The cubs were full of affection and demanded the same in return. It was love at first sight. David asked the boy if the pups were for sale. "Don't know," he said. "Come back tomorrow and talk to Al."

Early next morning Al was at the front gate giving instructions to his staff, and he beckoned for us to join the group. "Would you mind giving the boys a hand with a couple of the animals?" he asked David.

"I have to move a baby moose and two young camels from the barns into the pens." David readily agreed and jumped into the back of a small pickup. Sven and I watched the truck disappear in the direction of the barns and then turned toward the refreshment stand. "Hope he comes back with a wolf cub," I mumbled. It was our second day at the Game Farm, and we still didn't know if the cubs were for sale.

"You think we're crazy?" I asked my brother.

Sven shrugged. "Don't know." He took a sip of his Coke and studied the blue Alberta horizon.

David grinned and shook his head in disbelief. "You had me worried there for a while."

"Well, I tell you," Al began, "I've got just the four this year, and three of them have already been sold. Two are going to the Philadelphia Zoo, including the little female, and one is going to be shipped to San Diego. I was thinking of keeping the fourth for my boy—but I guess he can wait until next year."

Somehow, although the excitement so debilitated David that he could barely write the check to pay for Shunka, we managed to make arrangements with Al so that he would keep the wolf until we were back in Toronto. He promised he would pick out the gentlest of the cubs and fly him out to us. I asked Al if the wolf would have to be tranquilized.

"Nope," Al answered with a smile. "He's already tranquilized with love."

Before we left the Game Farm, we placed a call to Toronto. We shared a house with three other people and thought we should warn them of the imminent arrival of a wolf. Shoney answered the phone.

"You what!" he shouted at the other end of the line. "What the ... I don't believe it ... A wolf?... I don't believe it ... Yeah, well, okay. He's really small, eh?... Sure, sure, I'll tell the others. You're not putting me on, are you?... You're not, eh? A wolf. Too much," and he hung up.

We continued our trip west, and, in North Dakota, during a conversation with an Oglala Sioux, we discovered a name for our wolf. In the language of their people, the old man explained, the word for wolf was *Shun-Toksa*. Sometimes he was called *Shunka*—a sort of affectionate diminutive. The fact that Shunka also meant dog did not trouble us.

Three weeks later we were back in Toronto. Afraid that as Shunka grew older he would become less adaptable, we had dropped Sven in Cleveland and cut our trip short. It was another week, however, before we got our wolf cub. Alberta had been suffering through an intense heat wave and it was too hot for Shunka to withstand the fifty-mile drive from the Game Farm to the airport. Now, the long wait was over.

The rain began to ease up. I opened the car window and smelled the sweet rain-swept summer night. No sound other than the Rover's four-cylinder engine whining and vibrating along the expressway. I adjusted the rearview mirror, trying to focus on the wolf.

"How's he doing?" I asked.

"I think he's sleeping," David whispered. "My left arm is really tired from holding him, but I'm afraid if I move I'll wake him."

At the sound of our voices Shunka opened his eyes and sighed deeply, his little body shuddering as if some great sadness was sweeping through him. Then, resting his chin on David's forearm, he closed his eyes again and was lulled back to sleep by the sound of tires singing along wet pavement. A few more miles and he would be home.

Chapter 2

Home was a two-story, three-bedroom brick house that we shared with Ian, Shoney and Kathy. It was in a quiet family-oriented neighborhood where the lawns were always mowed and the hedges trimmed. One of the problems in sharing a house with other people was that no one could agree on whose turn it was to cut the grass and, as a result, the greenery in the backyard flourished unrestrained. Of the five people who had originally moved in, David and I were the only two who stayed out the one-year lease. Apparently the constant movement of people and changing faces unnerved our neighbors and counted as a definite strike two against us.

Strike one had already been chalked up when we moved in with twenty-one cats, five of which belonged to us. Although eleven of the twenty-one were newborn kittens and, therefore, not permanent residents, our neighbors were nevertheless unhappy, and our welcome had been a visit from the City Health Inspector. The man was apologetic looked around, declared the house remarkably clean, and left with two kittens for his grandchildren. Four months later, we gave away the rest of the cats. Shoney moved in and he was allergic to cat hair. Only Persephone remained, a tough, old New York alley cat who was to rule over Shunka as she did over the rest of the house.

We were sure Shunka's arrival would score us strike three, particularly when it were discovered he was a wolf. We had already checked with City Hall about the legality of keeping a wolf in the city and were advised that raising a wild animal native to Canada would require a special permit, the requirements of which were too complex to consider. In any case, with just a month left on our lease and intending to find a home outside the metropolitan area for ourselves and our menagerie, we decided to forgo that bureaucratic process. In the interest of keeping a low profile and not wishing to panic the neighbors, we agreed to pass Shunka off as a dog.

It had been a difficult decision inasmuch as it represented a contradiction. In raising Shunka we hoped to discredit some of the prejudices held against wolves. Yet now that we had him, these same prejudices forced us to lie about his identity. We consoled ourselves with the thought that it would be a temporary lie. Once we moved out of the city, we would drop the masquerade.

Shunka was happily accepted into our relaxed, disorganized household. As we pulled into the driveway with our baby wolf securely asleep in David's arms, Ian stood waiting on the front porch, eager to welcome Shunka home. He and Brian, a friend who had come by to celebrate the occasion, constituted the official reception committee.

David proudly carried Shunka into the house and put him down in the living room. Still dazed and disoriented, Shunka wandered aimlessly around the room, his tail tucked tightly between his legs and his head hung low. "He doesn't look at all vicious," Brian observed. "Not really what you'd expect a wolf to look like." Ian examined Shunka's skull and teeth and declared he looked like a little German shepherd puppy.

At the moment, more than anything else, Shunka looked lost and unhappy. Ignoring the four people who stared and poked at him, he sat down in a corner near the couch, and stretching out his huge paws, flopped over on his side. I shoved an old soft towel under him and patted his head. He acknowledged my presence with a soulful look and absently chewed a corner of the towel.

Like a couple of anxious parents coaxing a withdrawn and uncooperative child, David and I dangled rubber toys and stuffed animals in front of Shunka. We brought him water and tried to feed him. In our eagerness to make him happy, we overlooked the simple fact that Shunka was exhausted and probably suffering from mild shock as a result of his long journey into a strange and unfamiliar world. Naturally, all our attempts to bring him around met with failure. Shunka remained listless and continued to stare mournfully into the distance.

"Maybe we should play some wolf howls," I suggested, remembering an album David had bought for Shunka called "The Language and Music of the Wolves." Perhaps he would respond to the familiar sound of other wolves. David put the record on the turntable and soon the room echoed with a wide assortment of howls. Still no response from Shunka. When the shrill yapping of baby wolves carried through the speakers, he momentarily lifted his head to listen, but he seemed to know it wasn't the real thing and, with another heartfelt sigh, he resumed his attitude of disinterest.

Having tried everything to revive the little wolf, we called it a night. David made himself comfortable on the couch beside Shunka, and the little cub slept through without a sound. This peace was not to be a lasting one.

When I awoke the next morning, the house was bedlam. David and Shunka had been awake for some time, and the limp, lifeless little creature we had brought home turned into a whirlwind of destructive energy. His curiosity was overwhelming, and he seemed to get his teeth caught on anything within reach—bits and pieces of the morning paper were strewn throughout the house, someone's boot lay mangled in a corner, and Ian's cigarettes were quickly disappearing into Shunka's mouth. "He's hungry," David's voice called out as I tore the shredded cigarette package from Shunka's greedy jaws.

David was in the kitchen, surrounded by boxes of Pablum and

cans of evaporated milk. He was preparing Shunka's second meal of the day, and when I walked in, he was in the process of testing the temperature of the formula on his wrist. "Good grief," I mumbled, "it's like having a baby in the house." Shunka had to be fed six times a day and, fortunately, David took it upon himself to look after this tedious chore. At least the wolf didn't have to be bottle-fed. Al had weaned him at the Game Farm, and he happily slurped up his gruel from a flat, metal tray. The nice blue plastic dish we had bought for him was discarded after the first meal—Shunka had tried to devour it for dessert.

Still half-asleep, I stumbled around trying to get breakfast together. From the corner of my eye, I noticed Shunka edging toward the dining room, which was located off the kitchen. From his cautious approach, it was apparent he had not yet explored that part of the house. Then I remembered! Persephone had recently moved her kittens, and they were now under a low bench in the dining room. I quickly dropped my breakfast and grabbed Shunka as he was about to cross the threshold. Having more faith in the wolf's affectionate nature than I did, David suggested I put the cub down and see what happened. He was certain Shunka would not harm the kittens.

"Look at Persy," he argued, gesturing toward the large, white bovine cat sitting on the kitchen stool. "You know she would be in there with fur flying if she thought her kittens were in danger." I had to concede David's point and reluctantly put Shunka back down on the floor.

Persy (short for Persephone) was quite capable of looking after her young, and, at the moment, she seemed untroubled by Shunka's proximity to the dining room. A prolific kitten factory, Persephone had been around for a long time and was probably into her seventh life by the time Shunka arrived. She was a fearless old cat and had checked the wolf out earlier in the morning with a disdainful sniff and a properly intimidating swipe across his nose. Now that the newcomer had been put in his place, all was well in her world. Besides, it was feeding time and, having once had to fend for herself on the streets of New

York City where David and I had found her, Persy cherished nothing so much as her meals.

Shunka had meanwhile resumed his inspection of the dining room and had discovered the kittens. Puzzled by the squirming, furry little creatures, he picked up his ears and timidly strained his body forward to sniff them. Suddenly, before we realized what was happening, Persy flew across the room and raked a sharp claw strategically across the unwary wolf's nose. Shunka yelped and backed off. David grabbed Persy, and I quickly carried the box of kittens into our bedroom. After depositing them on the floor of our closet, I raced back downstairs to get Persy. I was too late. Having chased Shunka into the living room, Persephone had returned to her nest under the bench and discovered that her kittens had disappeared. To her mind, it was obvious the wolf had done away with them, and this time she was really going to get him.

She launched herself into Shunka with all four claws extended, yowling and spitting at him with murderous vengeance. Her tail was puffed into an angry plume and her entire body bristled with rage. David tried to disengage the furious cat from Shunka's fur, but she hung on tenaciously. After sustaining several injuries himself, David managed a firm hold on her and carried the ruffled cat upstairs to her kittens. She became instantly calm and fell to nursing her young.

Strangely, that day marked the beginning of Shunka's love affair with Persephone. Although wounded in pride as well as body for reasons he could never know, Shunka viewed Persy as an object to be worshipped. Persy had established her dominance over the wolf, and she remained dominant even after Shunka had grown into a rangy 130 pounds. Throughout their relationship, he always demonstrated unquestioning submission toward the old cat. With all the charm he could muster, he tirelessly courted her affection, humbly bowing and whimpering at her feet. Occasionally she permitted a few licks on top of her head, but for the most part, she ignored him or greeted him with a sharp right-hook to the nose. Persephone ruled and rightly so. Had she not established her dominance while Shunka was still a pup, once full grown, he could easily have killed her with a playful swipe of his huge paw.

Meanwhile, Persephone had completely demoralized the little pup. It had been evident from the time he awoke that Shunka missed the comfort and companionship of his brothers and sister. Despite his healthy appetite and energetic exploration of the house, he was periodically overcome by melancholia and stopped his play to emit a series of sad little whimpers. After Persy's severe chastisement, he became completely inconsolable and fell to pacing through the house, his moans and whimpers reaching such a pitiful crescendo that David and I briefly considered returning him to Al.

Under natural conditions, Shunka would have received large doses of affection daily from adult pack members. Now we had to replace this, and it didn't seem to be working. We stroked his head and scratched his belly, and David picked him up and carried him around the house as if he were a baby. All this attention provided only temporary relief. Shunka would soon become restless, and the pacing and crying began all over again. Nothing seemed to distract him from his song of woe— not the rubber mouse that squeaked, the doggy biscuits, nor the cuddly teddy bear. Nevertheless, a wolfish greed would not allow him to refuse any of the goodies offered him. By way of compromise, Shunka accepted each item and continued his lament while he gnawed and chewed—which at least reduced the shrill whimper to a low, throaty moan.

Al had suggested we raise Shunka with a dog—a furry, four-legged friend would keep him from getting lonely for his litter-mates and would also serve as a calming influence on the naturally high-strung wolf. We decided we had better get a dog fast. After a few phone calls, David came up with the name of someone on a farm who had a puppy to give away. She was from a litter of seven and the only one left. No one had wanted her because she was extremely quiet and lethargic. She sounded like the perfect playmate for Shunka, and we picked up Happy that afternoon.

It was a twenty-five-mile drive to the farm, and we took Shunka with us. If we accustomed him to traveling at an early age, we thought, Shunka would have no fear of the car and we could take him anywhere. The trip was a disaster.

Almost immediately, Shunka became carsick and frantically searched for an escape. Afraid he would jump out, we shut the windows of the car and watched helplessly as the hysterical wolf tried to bang and claw his way to freedom. The temperature was in the upper eighties and the stale, hot air in the Rover increased everyone's suffering.

Suddenly, Shunka stopped struggling and slumped to the floor, his heaving sides and drooling mouth the only indication that the limp little animal was still alive. Certain that he had collapsed from fright and heat exhaustion, I made David stop the car and climbed in back with Shunka. I stroked his near-lifeless body and gently coaxed him with a quiet, steady flow of words, but Shunka did not respond. We knew we had made a mistake in bringing him with us but, like the proverbial swimmer who suddenly tires in the middle of the lake, we had driven too far to turn back.

Although we were not aware of it at the time, Shunka's behavior was common to wolves in the wild. Once a wolf realizes he is trapped— particularly by man, his traditional enemy and overwhelming adversary—he will, in most cases, stop struggling and quietly await his fate. Biologists studying wolves in northern Canada discovered it was unnecessary to tranquilize a trapped wolf. By forcing the animal's neck down with a forked stick, they were able to ear-tag him, fasten a radio collar around his neck and examine his teeth. Throughout this activity, the wolf was as docile as if anesthetized.

It was a relief to pull into the farmhouse driveway. Two huge Newfoundland dogs as large as cows sat under a gnarled old tree in the dusty front yard. A young barefoot man appeared from behind the house and, after preliminary introductions, he presented us with Hammer—a little moplike dog with long black hair, white chest and paws, and sad brown eyes. We immediately renamed her Happy.

She calmly accepted our offer of friendship and politely returned our advances with a few affectionate licks. Although a puppy, Happy was a serious dog. Unlike Shunka, who would continue to change dramatically, Happy would always look as she did that day. Only her size changed.

As we headed toward the car, Happy didn't even look back at her 250-pound Newfoundland father or petite Border collie mother, but nestled peacefully in David's arms, gazing at him with solemn trusting eyes. All she wanted out of life was love and a chance to serve her master.

The young man followed us to the car to see what a wolf looked like. We had not told him over the telephone that Happy was to be playmate and companion to an arctic wolf pup, and he seemed hesitant as he peered at Shunka's inanimate body. "I guess he'll be all right if you don't let him get out of hand," he said, eyeing the wolf suspiciously.

"There's nothing to worry about," David assured him. "He's really quite gentle."

"Can't say as I'd want to raise one. I've raised a lot of dogs, but I sure wouldn't want to mess with a wolf."

This conversation was typical of many we would have as we grew with Shunka. "I'd sooner trust a wolf than a Doberman or a shepherd," David replied, but the remark was ignored by our friend. As I climbed into the Rover, he shut the door after me and leaned in. "Just make sure you keep him in line," he said. "Slap him hard if he doesn't obey you—it's the one thing they understand."

We assumed he was talking about Shunka, although that might have explained why Happy was so meek and docile. "People just don't like wolves," I observed as we headed home with one sick wolf and a friendly, relaxed Happy dog.

Chapter 3

Despite the dramatic and convincing performance of "Trapped Wolf Dying" that Shunka had given in the car, he survived the trip. In fact, given his previous limp and lifeless image, his instantaneous recovery was amazing. The minute David put him down inside the hallway, it was as if someone had tapped the wolf with a magic wand, and, like Sleeping Beauty in the fairy tale, he came back to life. Without a moment's hesitation, he flung himself upon an unwary Happy.

Whether he had been aware of the dog's presence during the ride home and stored the information in his mind until the ordeal was over, or whether he noticed her for the first time at that moment was difficult to tell—but in any case, he now eagerly proceeded to impress upon her the lupine ritual of dominance. Although Shunka's movements lacked some of the dignity we had witnessed among Al Oeming's wolves, the basic motions expressing dominance were unmistakably the same. With tail erect and ears pointed forward, Shunka firmly fixed his jaws around Happy's neck, at which point she was supposed to either fight for supremacy or throw herself on her back, exposing her jugular vein to the triumphant wolf in a plea for mercy. Presumably Shunka would then stand nobly over her prostrate body and proclaim his position as the alpha wolf. However, Happy didn't know any of this and, shaking herself free from Shunka's grasp, showed complete disinterest in his ritualistic game. Shunka seemed momentarily baffled but, undaunted and high of spirit, he turned and rammed into the unsuspecting dog—apparently reasoning that if he couldn't threaten her into submission, he would physically force her into the position. His efforts again met with failure. Happy was built like a tank—sturdy and solid, her center of gravity close to the ground. She was also heavier than Shunka, weighing in at twenty-seven pounds, compared to his twenty. This imbalance would reverse itself as they grew older, but, unless he caught her off-guard, Shunka would always find it difficult to up-end the firmly entrenched dog.

The little routine in the hall seemed to go on forever. Shunka was determined and persistent. Happy was good-natured and tolerant. Ian suggested that perhaps she was merely stupid, but I dismissed his suggestion, replying that it took character to withstand such tedious bullying without resorting to physical battle. Happy did have her limits, however, and eventually her patience gave out. Assuming an attitude of quiet resolve, she turned to face the overzealous wolf cub and, with lowered head, she plowed into his side. The surprised wolf hit the floor, spindly legs helplessly pawing the air. For the time being, the contest was over, and the pups fell to playful wrestling. Although it had not yet been established who was the boss, the friendship between the two animals was firmly sealed. We were relieved. Happy was a successful addition to the household and an instant cure for Shunka's homesickness.

The rest of the day continued on a merry and somewhat frenzied note. It was open house as friends and acquaintances dropped in to meet the wolf. Shunka took well to his new-found celebrity status, and from that first day he exhibited a natural ability to ham it up, look adorable and generally win friends and influence people.

His eagerness to give and receive love was for me a strong denial of the popular concept that a wolf is, by instinct, a wanton and vicious killer. Like any other animal, a wolf is, by instinct, a survivor. Killing is a necessary tool for his survival and not a sporting activity nor an amusing diversion. At eight weeks, protectively watched by his parents or other pack members (adult wolves are extremely tolerant and fond of young pups and "babysitting" is a common phenomenon in most packs), a young wolf pup spends his time playing and exploring the area around the den site. Predatory activities such as pouncing, ripping and tearing are very much evident during this play and develops the faculties necessary for him to become an efficient and effective hunter. But, unless he learns how to hunt with the rest of the pack, his chances for survival in the wilderness are slim. Adult animals have learned to divide the living world into three categories—predator, prey and equal. A young cub doesn't make these distinctions and therefore doesn't know which animals to run from, which animals to attack and which animals to play with. Consequently, he welcomes all outsiders into his territory with curiosity, playfulness and an open attitude which says, "If you love me, I'll love you back."

In this respect Shunka's behavior was no different from that of his brothers and sisters in the wilderness. Most visitors were greeted with eager wolf-kisses which, unlike a dog's licking, consisted of a series of quick flicks of the tongue. Mike and Hyla, who were the first recipients that afternoon of Shunka's enthusiastic greeting, brought with them an elegantly hand-painted sign that read "Beware of Wolf." Given the circumstances, it was unanimously agreed the sign should be relettered to read "Beware of Affectionate Wolf." It took patience and forbearance to withstand Shunka's greetings, but no one seemed to mind. The only objection came from Happy. The unassuming, good-natured puppy was suddenly overcome by jealousy. Emitting a tortured half growl, half shriek, she tore loose from Mike who had been scratching her belly and catapulted herself onto the couch and into Hyla's lap, which was not very big and had already been claimed by Shunka. Hyla disappeared beneath the two furry bodies as they struggled and fought for her attention.

Happy's reaction was inexplicable. She had not been ignored in favor of the wolf and had seemed content with Mike's admiration while Hyla played with Shunka. But jealousy was the motivating factor, and it was an emotion that would continue to besiege her whenever people came to see the wolf. We had anticipated this problem when we decided to take Happy, knowing that because Shunka was a wolf, he would be the center of attention and Happy would feel rejected. We agreed on a policy of equal treatment for both animals under all circumstances and impressed this upon everyone who came to visit.

Despite our efforts to avoid favoritism, Happy sensed that somehow Shunka was special, that there was something about him that elicited a stronger response from people than her own gentle demeanor. She must have observed Shunka's aggressive behavior in greeting visitors and decided that this was the way it was to be done. In fact, she not only adopted his energetic style with guests but expanded it to such a degree that she became difficult to deal with. She hurled herself at people with a furious determination to divert any and all attention away from Shunka, and in her desperate attempt, grabbed mouthfuls of hair or beard, causing pain when she meant to express love. She also made her sense of frustration known to Shunka by knocking him down, sinking her teeth into his ruff or tail and growling at him. Shunka seemed to have no idea what it was all about and tolerated Happy's punishment, accepting it as playful roughhousing. In fact, halfway through the tussle, Happy seemed to forget the reason for her displeasure, and the battle ended up a gleeful wrestling match. This behavior was to become routine, but that afternoon we were not expecting such a vehement display of sibling rivalry.

Peace was restored after Mike and Hyla left—but not for long. The pups barely had time to finish their mid-afternoon Pablum before Wendy, a former member of the household, arrived bearing gifts of juicy raw bones. Shunka must have smelled the bones coming up the street. He was at the front door and ready to greet Wendy before she was in the house. Fortunately Wendy is a stalwart and unflappable individual, because, unfortunately, she arrived wearing shorts. The minute she stepped inside the door, she was overwhelmed by two pups fighting for her attention. Shunka was driven to an even greater display of wolfish enthusiasm by the contents of the paper bag she carried. He jumped around ecstatically, sharp wolf claws raking bare legs as he strained toward the bag, eager tongue licking her arms and hands as she reached out to scratch his head.

"He's really friendly, isn't he," she said, hardly flinching as the welts on her legs multiplied.

David picked up Shunka to rescue Wendy from the cub's welcome, at the same time giving Happy a chance to say hello. Shunka squirmed and whined and fought heroically to break loose and get back to Wendy. "He seems to like you," David observed.

Wendy laughed and headed for the kitchen. David put the wriggling wolf back on the floor, and Shunka immediately made a beeline for Wendy. Again he threw himself at her, joyfully licking her hands and legs and whining excitedly.

"What is in that bag, Wendy?" I asked, noticing that the object under her arm was the focus of Shunka's attention.

"Bones," she said, and suddenly grasping the situation, she burst out laughing. "No wonder he's so attracted to me."

As soon as she reached into the bag and took out one of the bones, pandemonium prevailed. In one unbroken move, Shunka grabbed it from her hand and scrambled out the back door. We were a little startled by his voracious behavior but shrugged it off as wolfish greed. We were soon to find out just how inspiring wolfish greed could be. Shunka must have sensed that there was more in the bag than he had in his mouth. With uncannily perfect timing, he dashed back inside just as Wendy was offering the second bone to Happy, swiped it from her hand and ran back out. The situation required human intervention if Happy was to get her share of the treats. David retrieved one of the bones from the yard and gave it to the bewildered dog. She accepted it very delicately and then stood blinking and thinking, presumably trying to decide what to do with it or where to take it. She didn't have much time. Shunka reappeared at the door, his mouth bulging with the bone allotted him and his eyes coveting the bone in Happy's mouth. He was now faced with a dilemma. He had to protect his own bone and at the same time get Happy's. Reluctantly he dropped his trophy, and keeping a protective paw on top of it, leaned over and closed his jaws around the piece protruding from Happy's mouth. He growled and tugged until Happy released her grip. The bone was Shunka's. I could not let this injustice continue, and reached toward the bone Shunka had been forced to abandon. My movement did not go unnoticed. Shunka swung around, snarled very sincerely and lunged for the bone I had tried to pick up.

"David, I think he means business," I mumbled. The sudden change in Shunka's behavior was beginning to unnerve me.

"This is ridiculous," David said. "He's still a pup, a baby. He's just making a lot of noise and being greedy." With this assessment of the situation, David picked up Happy and one of the bones and took the dog into the dining room. He stationed himself in the doorway to make sure Shunka could not torment the dog while she gnawed her bone.

Shunka accepted his defeat and settled down to his own bone, his chewing and ripping accompanied by deep, throaty growls. To let him know that there were no hard feelings, I bent down to pat his head. Shunka snarled and moved out of arm's reach. I looked at David. This wasn't supposed to happen. David walked over to the preoccupied wolf and kneeling down, softly spoke to him. Shunka responded with more growling and snapping, this time showing an impressive display of sharp baby fangs. Our friendly, affectionate wolf had become a snarling little tyrant.

"Why don't you let him finish it and then see how he is," Wendy suggested, while Shunka continued to gnaw and softly growl to himself.

David and I were extremely troubled. We had been advised by self-appointed experts that one should never give raw meat to a wild animal. "It will make him vicious and he might turn on you," they had said. We hadn't believed that old wives' tale, but now faced with a menacing little terror who would not even permit a friendly scratch of his head, we wondered if perhaps there was something to the story. Angry and frustrated by this ridiculous situation, I impulsively plucked the bone from between Shunka's paws. My movement was so quick and unexpected, and probably naive and stupid, that before Shunka realized what had happened, the bone was in David's hands.

"Get it out of here," I said, suddenly shaken by what I had done and the thought of what Shunka could have done. His baby teeth were needle sharp and his jaws were already strong enough to have cracked the disputed bone.

"I think from now on we should boil any bones we give them," David said and, picking up Happy's bone, he dropped both of them into a large pot of hot water.

Now that the bones were gone for good, like a Dr. Jekyll and Mr. Hyde character, Shunka reverted to his former loving self. He and Happy enjoyed a luxurious belly rub and after acknowledging Wendy's admiration with a few more wolf kisses and dog licks, the two of them curled up together in the dining room to resume their afternoon nap. The contested bones were later returned to them, well boiled, and Shunka gnawed his with only slightly more interest than he devoted to his rubber and rawhide toys.

David and I were still upset by the little scene that had taken place, and I apologized to Wendy for Shunka's ungracious behavior. Wendy didn't think the incident was particularly unusual. "Do you think he would have bitten you?" she asked, noticing the anxiety in our faces.

That was the problem. We didn't know, and we didn't know how to find out. There was not much recorded information on raising wolves in captivity, and much less about raising wolves in your house.

Wendy suggested a vet. That brought up another problem. Both animals needed their rabies shots and a checkup. We had tried and failed to locate a veterinarian who was willing to take a wolf as a client. It was, however, understandable that we had been turned down by a number of clinics. Worried that someone might react negatively to our raising a wolf in captivity and possibly alert City Hall, David had been very secretive and noncommittal on the telephone. More often than not, I am sure the party on the other end of the line figured the call for a practical joke. Wendy gave us the name of her animal clinic. One of the doctors had raised a wildcat and, we hoped, we would meet with less skepticism. David immediately placed the call. His voice wavered momentarily on the word "wolf," and then he relaxed. The woman on the phone didn't laugh or question his credibility. She merely took down the necessary information and made an appointment for Happy and Shunka.

The heat of the August afternoon had settled heavily inside the house and we sought relief in the yard. We settled down among the tall weeds and grasses with ice-cold lemonade, a couple of wolf books— and Wendy with her knitting. Even Persephone joined us and, after digging an earth-cool hole for herself beneath a bush, she dozed with one eye trained on the house.

Our golden hour of peace passed quickly and soon two sleepy little pups appeared on the back porch. It didn't take long for Shunka to notice Persephone, and this realization instantly revived him. He tumbled down the half-dozen steps and bounded toward the sleepy cat, squeaking his love and delight. The thorny bush provided a perfect shield, and all Shunka could do was press his face close to the ground and lovingly peer at Persy. The courtship might have continued for the rest of the afternoon but it was interrupted by the unexpected appearance of a large, white German shepherd known as Mushka. The owners of the dog—who had been responsible for our finding Happy—followed a few steps behind. Shunka's preference for four-footed friends was made evident by the fact that he ignored the two human visitors but frantically fawned over their dog. Mushka was about five years old and rather matronly. She had had a litter of pups before being spayed and now had no patience with a squirming wolf pup who insisted on mistaking her for his mother. We had seen Shunka express excitement in greeting new visitors and had witnessed his avid courtship of Persy, but this was different. He approached the older dog extremely submissively, crawling on his stomach while squeaking and whimpering, or rolling over on his back in front of her. Whenever he could get close enough, he nibbled her muzzle and licked her face.

This type of behavior is common among young wolves toward their mothers or older pack members. The nipping and licking of the muzzle stimulates the older wolf to regurgitate freshly eaten semidigested food which is then immediately devoured by the young. According to L. David Mech's *The Wolf,* this food-begging ritual is similar to and possibly instrumental in teaching a young pup active submission. Adult wolves have been observed to employ the same patterns of behavior in approaching an alpha wolf.

Unfortunately, Shunka was unable to communicate his intentions to Mushka. His solicitation merely provoked her anger, and she bared her fangs and growled a warning. Instead of frightening Shunka, the dog's hostility rallied him to greater efforts. There was no way for Mushka to avoid the little wolf, and, out of exasperation, she snapped at him. We were quickly assured by her owners that Mushka would not hurt Shunka, but we were not convinced. Mushka had never before had to deal with a wolf cub, so who could predict what she would do if Shunka pushed her too far? Finally, at the risk of insulting our guests, David asked that the dog be removed. Shunka whimpered pitifully as Mushka was led away. They were to meet again some months later, but their next meeting would be very different.

Once Mushka was out of sight, Shunka turned his full attention to the people in the yard. Mushka's owner was a quiet, gentle person, and we were surprised when he knocked Shunka on his back, playfully batted his nose and roughly rolled the pup from side to side on the grass. David quickly intervened, pointing out that Shunka was, after all, a wolf and required gentle handling. The roughhousing eased up, but only for a few minutes. Shunka was soon off his feet again and playfully tossed around.

"I'm not hurting him," our friend assured us. "I play like this with Mushka all the time, and she loves it."

Another misconception in man's dealing with wolves became apparent. Of those who did not view the animal as a treacherous villain, a significant percentage insisted on lumping the wolf together with dogs and handled him accordingly. It was difficult to make him understand that wolves don't react well to being manhandled by people. Shunka and Happy might happily roughhouse with each other, wolves within a pack might wrestle together, but it is not acceptable for a person to take such physical liberties with a wolf—at least, not with Shunka. He was not reacting well to the rough treatment he was getting. After several attempts to solicit what a wolf might consider a properly affectionate greeting and finding himself instead tossed around like a sack of flour, Shunka lost interest completely in his guest and turned to torment Happy.

There was no way to demand Shunka's attention and affection. It was a gift he bestowed upon you—on his own terms. We were aware wolves had a healthy mistrust of mankind and knew that Shunka would tolerate little abuse from people. Our worry was not that he would become vicious and wild, but that he would retreat in fear and withdraw the affection he gave so easily. As evening drew near and our guests departed, David and I reproached ourselves for not having been more firm about how Shunka was handled by others. So far, Shunka had accepted us. This tenuous bond of friendship was more important than wounded egos, and we vowed it would not happen again.

Dinner presented a new problem. Happy and Shunka couldn't be left unsupervised in the open yard while we ate, so we brought them inside. How unrealistic of us to think we could enjoy a peaceful dinner while a wolf roamed freely about the dining room! Although too little to reach the table top, Shunka nevertheless made his presence felt. He stepped on toes, leaned against legs, pawed at laps and attached his teeth to clothing demanding that he be noticed. Goaded on by Shunka's activities, Happy was as pesky as the wolf. David finally had no choice but to take them back outside and chain them up on two stakes he had screwed into the ground.

He had barely finished a chicken leg when a hair-raising shriek and steady wailing echoed from the yard. Bolting out of his chair,

David rushed to the window. Happy and Shunka had neatly entwined their chains together and, standing neck to neck, loudly complained of their plight. They became very quiet while David patiently picked at the ten feet of knotted chain, and when he finally had them untangled, both pups gently licked his hands in gratitude. However, as soon as he turned back toward the house, the howling and yowling began again in earnest. They were tangled again before David could sit down at the table. I had been watching the proceedings from the window, between mouthfuls of dinner, and it was obvious that the second entanglement was deliberate. Shunka and Happy had figured out a clever way to get attention. Throughout the duration of the meal, the pups became tangled around trees, bushes and each other, and David, Wendy and I finished dinner on the run, taking turns untangling the snarled chains.

It was not the most relaxing meal I can remember, and we finished it quickly so that the animals could be released from their temporary imprisonment. I could almost see indignant tears in Shunka's and Happy's eyes as they trotted back into the house. They sniffed the dining room thoroughly to see what they had missed, but everything had been cleared away and the room was once again a barren "animal den."

There was no rug on that floor and little furniture beyond a table, chairs and a wooden bench, so therefore—except for dinner time—it had been designated the animals' room. Shunka and Happy did have access to the kitchen, but since all the counters were beyond their reach there was nothing there for them to destroy. The rest of the house was conveniently blocked off by a four-foot-high movable sheet of plywood.

Before bedtime, we placed a blanket on the dining room floor to serve as a bed for Shunka and Happy. Shunka, however, immediately claimed the large red blanket as his own. Whenever Happy trotted over to lie down on it, he grabbed one end with his teeth and dragged it away, pulling it out from under the dog, who was too good-natured to fight for her rights. He stuffed the blanket into a corner, plopped down on it and gathered all the loose corners about him so there was no room for Happy. We tried to coax him into sharing it without success, so we sacrificed another blanket and presented it to Happy. Before the poor dog could get settled on the new spread, Shunka darted out and pulled that too from under her and stashed it with the first blanket. We tried again, this time with an old towel, but Shunka would not allow it. It seemed this was one battle Happy would have to fight for herself, but she chose to forgo the comfort of a blanket and stretched out on the barren floor. Shunka looked disappointed. After fidgeting on top of his pile, he picked up the red blanket and dragged it to Happy's end of the room. He dropped it in front of her and lay down beside the dog.

We began to learn that Shunka was not as greedy as he appeared. He was expressing his dominance—a status he seemed to have gained by default since Happy didn't care—and like any alpha wolf, he insisted on his right to decide what was to be shared and how. If he felt Happy should have something, he ceremoniously presented it to her. Occasionally Happy challenged his decisions, but most of the time, she went along with his rules.

Between the ages of three and eleven weeks, a young wolf's emotional ties need constant reinforcement. In the wild, the pack structure is formed during this period of his life. As part of Shunka's socialization program and to strengthen the bond between them, David decided to sleep in the dining room with the animals. At least for the first week.

Newspapers were spread out on the floor, and David rolled out his sleeping bag. I agreed with this plan in principle, as long as I didn't have to participate. Selfishly I opted for the comfort of my bed, leaving David to deal with the trials and discomforts of sleeping with a wolf. Actually, there was very little sleeping done in the dining room that night. Happy and Shunka took little series of naps, each lasting about an hour or two. The time between naps was spent in wrestling, chewing the foam pad beneath David's sleeping bag and mauling David with affection.

David tried to adapt himself to this method of sleep. He had once read that that was how wolves slept and that it was in fact very healthy and restful. Between siestas he picked up soiled newspapers, mopped the floor as needed and played with the animals. By morning, he realized that only wolf cubs, puppies, babies and possibly mothers and madmen madmen could function on such a time schedule. It didn't work for an adult human being who had to stay awake all day. David was exhausted, and as soon as I came down to report for duty, he climbed upstairs to bed.

Chapter 4

I was sitting in my favorite spot in the yard—a broken-down wooden bench protected by a wooden canopy, once painted white and now sheltered from the sun by an ivy shroud—reading the paper and watching Shunka and Happy splashing in their water basin. The screen door slammed, and David appeared, blinking into the sunlight, two chains dangling from his hands.

"I'm going to give the animals their first lesson in leash walking," he announced.

"Don't you think you're rushing it a little," I said. "Shunka has only been here two days—give him a little more time to adjust."

"He's doing fine," David answered, and walked to the large rectangular container which was usually filled with fresh drinking water for the pups but at the moment contained a wet dog. While Shunka didn't share Happy's love for bathing, he seemed content to amuse himself by pawing as much water out of the basin as possible with his front feet. He did surprisingly well, and as streams of water sparkled into the air and sloshed over the edge, Happy soon found herself sitting in nothing more than a puddle of muddy water. His objective accomplished, Shunka gleefully turned to David, jumping against his legs and clamoring for attention. David scooped the cub into his arms and hugged him, letting the wolf cover his face with kisses and gently nibble his nose. Watching Shunka nuzzling David's face, I was reminded of the wolf's behavior toward the dog Mushka, although in this instance Shunka was relaxed and there was no frantic whining and squirming. This form of expression apparently had a function other than as an exercise in passive submission and as a food-begging ritual—it was also simply a demonstration of affection.

Once the hugging and loving was dispensed with, it was playtime. David took a rawhide bone from his pocket, stuck it in his mouth and took off down the length of the yard on his hands and knees, Shunka and Happy loping and bouncing beside him trying to fix their teeth on the prize. "Part of David's socialization program for Shunka," I thought as I watched the ridiculous spectacle. Everything David did, he did thoroughly. Once committed to an idea, he directed all his thoughts and energies toward the object of interest—sometimes to the point of wearing out everyone else around him. And so it was with Shunka. The wolf was a consuming passion, and he did everything in his power to understand the animal and relate to him on the wolf's terms. Shunka was responding well, and despite my anxiety that David was expecting too much from the little cub, the pup didn't seem bothered at all. The galloping party reached my end of the yard, and David relinquished the piece of rawhide to Shunka, taking a second one from his pocket for Happy.

"Where's Ian?" he asked as he sprawled beside me on the bench.

"He went to buy lumber for the dog house," I answered absently. Ian, who made his living as a silversmith, was equally adept with carpentry tools and had offered to build a house for Shunka and Happy. The plan called for cedar planks and cedar shingles, and room enough for dog and wolf. All in all it was going to be the finest dog house ever built, and it was our hope that, once it was completed, Shunka would make himself at home in it and the rest of us could recover full use of the dining room.

"Time for the walk," David said and got up to snap the leashes on Shunka and Happy. "Why don't you come along? You can take Happy."

We didn't get very far. In fact, we didn't move at all. Neither animal budged as we tugged on their chains. Happy looked at me sadly, unsure of what it was I wanted her to do. Shunka perhaps understood even less than Happy what was expected of him, but one thing he had no doubts about—he was not going to get up and walk merely because David wished him to do so. Instead, he sat down and, planting his front paws firmly into the ground, complacently looked at the big hairy human tugging on his leash and coaxing him with pleading words, "Come on Shunka. Come here Shunka." Shunka cocked his head at David, stretched out on his stomach and suddenly took great interest in sniffing the patch of grass in front of him. We next tried the front sidewalk, hoping the new surroundings would arouse curiosity and compel the pups to walk on their own, no matter in what direction. We guessed wrong, and after dragging two miserable and reluctant creatures a few feet down the sidewalk, the lesson was temporarily abandoned.

At least neither animal seemed to object to the leash itself, which was a beginning, and important, because later that day Shunka and Happy were scheduled for their first visit to the vet. And even if they would not cooperate by walking at the end of a chain, David would at least have some control over them.

As in most ventures that required moving Shunka from one place to another by automobile, the occasion did not pass without a minor crisis. At the time, however, we expected behavior no more dramatic than the pitiable resignation we had witnessed during previous drives, and consequently, it was decided that David could handle the trip without my help. The details of that adventure were related to me that evening while dog and wolf slept peacefully in the shadow of an azalea bush.

"You will be happy to know," David informed me, "that Shunka did not panic in the car. He didn't pant, drool or play dead. In fact, he was extremely curious about the whole thing and seemed to be having a good time." He paused a moment and sipped from the bottle of soda in his hand. "The bad news is that I almost lost him out the back window."

Unlike most car windows which roll up and down, the Land Rover windows slide open sideways, but they move back and forth in notches and cannot be slid open without manually releasing the spring which locks them into each notch. Therefore, I couldn't understand how Shunka could have pushed his way out the window. "What do you mean, *lost* him?" I asked.

"He jumped out," David replied and proceeded with the story. He had left the back side windows open a few inches for air, and somehow, Shunka managed to squeeze himself through. Perhaps the notches had slipped, but in any case, David looked back and saw Shunka dangling by his knees out of the right rear window, somewhat resembling a wolf pelt strapped to the side of the car—except that this one was alive. He grabbed the wolf's tail and desperately looked for a sidestreet, praying that the movement of the Rover would keep Shunka from jumping. Traffic was heavy and he didn't dare stop on the main road for fear that Shunka would be hit by another car. With Happy playfully nibbling his ears, one hand on the steering wheel and the other clutching a squirming wolf, David finally pulled into a quiet deadend street. As soon as the car stopped, Shunka jumped. His freedom, however, was shortlived. David was out of the car almost as fast as Shunka, and the rumpled wolf was quickly deposited back in the car, the windows were closed and the journey continued.

If David had been badly shaken by the experience, Shunka seemed to suffer no ill effects from his crazy stunt ride and, upon arriving at the vet's office, he was eager to explore his surroundings with his usual exuberance.

Except for David and his menagerie, the waiting room was empty. To avoid undue alarm among regular patrons, the appointment had been wisely scheduled for after business hours. Shunka would have been delighted to find himself in a room full of cats and dogs and people, but one can only imagine the mayhem he would have caused with his dogmatic insistence upon proper lupine etiquette.

"You must be Mr. Ostriker." A woman dressed in starched white had appeared from one of the examination rooms and approached David. "And this must be the wolf puppy," she said as Shunka strained on his leash to greet Elizabeth, who could have doubled for Katharine Hepburn. It was Elizabeth who had made the appointment, and we were eventually to realize that it was Elizabeth who was responsible for the smooth and efficient operation of the clinic. She remembered names, the animals that belonged to the names, and the stories that belonged to each animal.

Years later, she recounted the prelude to Shunka's first visit to the clinic. Apparently, David's remark over the telephone that Shunka was a wolf had been calmly received because past experience had taught Elizabeth that the odds on a real wolf showing up were practically nil. When Elizabeth informed Dr. Suzi Francis and her associate, Dr. Reeve-Newson, that their new patient was a wolf, they too had expressed skepticism. "We've heard that one before," Dr. Reeve-Newson had chuckled, and Dr. Francis echoed his doubt. "I'll believe it when I see it," she had said. That Shunka turned out to be the real thing surprised and delighted everyone.

The fact was, by the time David arrived at the clinic, we were no longer completely convinced that Shunka really was pure wolf. Everyone who met him insisted he looked like a German shepherd puppy. Never having seen a wolf cub other than Shunka and his siblings at the Game Farm, we began to suffer moments of uncertainty. Wasn't it possible, we wondered, that Shunka's mother could have mated with a dog, as wolves have been known to do? Was it possible to determine whether an animal was a full-blooded wolf before he reached maturity, and if so, how? These musings reflected our ignorance about the animal we had adopted, and our doubts certainly didn't do justice to Al Oeming and his vast knowledge of wildlife. However, we were just beginning to learn—and one of the things we wanted to find out was what exactly distinguished a wolf from a dog.

David was filling out the record cards Elizabeth had given him when Dr. Francis came out and introduced herself. She looked at

Shunka but did not comment on his "wolfness." David hoisted him onto the shiny metal table, and Dr. Francis carefully explored the formation of Shunka's skull, his teeth, jawline and body structure.

"He certainly is a wolf," she finally announced and explained that the most significant criterion in distinguishing a wolf from a dog is the axis of a wolf's eyes. Also known as the orbital angle, it is the degree of the angle formed by a line drawn through the outer edges of the eye socket and another across the top of the skull. In wolves, this angle measures approximately 40 to 45 degrees, while it is considerably wider in dogs.

Dr. Reeve-Newson came into the examination room to meet Shunka. Through the coming year, he and Dr. Francis would be responsible for Shunka's medical welfare, and it was important that they both form a relationship with him at this early stage. According to a number of studies, after the approximate age of twenty weeks, a wolf will have firmly established his social ties and will more than likely reject strangers, a problem we did not want to face in the future whenever Shunka required medical attention. It was a relief to find two doctors not only willing to accept Shunka as a regular client, but who also took a personal interest in the wolf.

David's list of wolf diseases and vaccinations was superfluous since Dr. Francis obviously knew her business. She proceeded with Shunka's distemper shot, explaining that wolves required an attenuated, live-virus vaccination, which was slightly more painful than that administered to dogs. Shunka, however, didn't seem to notice the shot and cheerfully showered Dr. Francis with wolf kisses. Surprisingly, Happy was the more reluctant patient, attempting to slink off the table and leaning against David to show her displeasure at the proceedings.

"One more thing," David said as I stood up and began collecting plates and pop bottles scattered about the yard. "I picked up some raw bones on the way home. I asked Dr. Francis about it and she said raw meat will not turn Shunka 'wild.'" Dr. Francis had explained to David that Shunka's behavior had been natural—he was protecting his claim to a choice meal, and when we tried to take it away, he reacted like any other animal whose territorial rights were invaded. Just as one should never take a bone away from a dog without expecting the animal's active disapproval, one should never disturb a wolf absorbed in his meal. So much for the "raw-meat-equals-vicious-wolf" theory.

Dusk had slowly crept around us while we talked, and refreshed by their naps, Shunka and Happy were busily snuffling around the yard. We sat quietly for a few minutes and watched Shunka pouncing on grasshoppers and searching out the crickets who had made our heavily foliated yard their evening concert hall. His futile efforts were comical to watch. Front paws spread awkwardly apart and nose close to the ground, he stared intently into the grass. Suddenly spotting movement, he reared up on his hind legs and lunged down upon his intended prey, which, by the time he made contact with the ground, was more than likely halfway across the neighbor's yard. Often, the pounces ended with Shunka sprawled ungracefully on the grass—he was still gangly and awkward and his sense of balance had not yet fully developed.

He had worked his way toward the area behind the garage where, earlier in the summer, Wendy had dug up the earth for a garden which never materialized. But you might say her work was not a total loss. Persephone had claimed it as her spacious outdoor litter box. As Shunka stepped into the black square of dirt, nose leading the way, he seemed to forget the grasshopper hunt and stood frozen with his right paw in mid-air. Suddenly he became animated with intense excitement, frantically sniffing and snuffling the loose earth. Then, with left shoulder leading, he bent toward the ground and rolled luxuriously in the dirt, his feet lazily pawing the air.

I suggested to David that perhaps that wasn't the best place for Shunka to be rolling around. He agreed and started toward the wolf. As soon as Shunka saw him coming, he scrambled to his feet, shook himself from nose to tail and raced toward the house. Much to our chagrin, he had uncovered fresh animal droppings and had recognized that the odor was related to Persephone. Rolling in her smell was Shunka's adaption of a common lupine hunting tactic. After a kill, a wolf will sometimes break open the urinary gland of the dead animal and roll around in it. He will then smell like the prey species and can hope to approach his next quarry undetected, possibly assuring himself of another meal.

Shunka's motives, however, were much less sinister. Still unsuccessful in his courtship of Persy, something from his dim, inherited past urged him to roll in her droppings—the logic being that if he smelled like a cat, Persy would naturally accept him. Looking very pleased with himself, he scrambled up the porch steps and submissively approached the cat stationed in the doorway. Persy was disgusted. She hissed, turned her back on him and trotted back into the house. Shunka was perplexed by her rejection and pursued her inside, there to be met by Kathy and Shoney, who had just returned home from a summer of building log cabins in the north and had yet to make Shunka's acquaintance.

Before Shunka could jump on the horrified newcomers, David dragged the stinking, filthy wolf outside and thoroughly hosed him down, grumbling and muttering as he fumbled around in the dark. Now that Shunka had discovered this new tactic of rolling, it was the first of many distasteful baths for the wolf. Fortunately, he also discovered smells less offensive and delighted in rolling on banana peels, cigars, and people wearing perfume.

Washed, brushed and combed, Shunka was reintroduced to Kathy and Shoney. They too would be sharing the house with the animals, and it was important that Shunka and Happy make a good impression, particularly since Kathy and Shoney's first meeting with the wolf had happened under unfavorable circumstances.

During Shunka's bath, Happy had already curried Kathy's favor, which was not difficult since Kathy had grown up with a gigantic, cuddly Newfoundland dog to whom Happy bore some resemblance. That Kathy actually favored Happy over Shunka was a small victory for the dog. For once it was Shunka who was fighting to get attention, while Happy possessively snuggled closer to Kathy. It wasn't much of a battle. Jealousy was a trait foreign to Shunka's personality, and having elicited an affectionate welcome from Kathy, he was satisfied.

Shoney, on the other hand, wasn't sure how to react to either animal, and after politely and cautiously patting each of them on the head, he disappeared into his room. From that first meeting no one could have guessed Shoney would become one of Shunka's favorite people, and that he in turn would tolerate affectionate mauling and playful teasing from the wolf above and beyond normal human endurance. The fact was, beneath it all, Shoney was a soft touch, which became obvious the following morning when we found him standing on the kitchen stool, Shunka pawing at his feet and Happy staring up at him with sad, liquid eyes.

"Do something," Shoney yelled as David slid aside the plywood board and entered the kitchen. "I'm trying to eat breakfast and I think they want it. Maybe they're hungry—why don't you give them something to eat."

The animals were not hungry. David had stumbled down two hours earlier and had fed them. Nevertheless, both dog and wolf were always ready to eat, particularly if the food belonged to someone else. It was a funny-sad predicament for Shoney. He always had his breakfast in the kitchen, and it had not occurred to him to escape into the living room with his peanut butter and jelly sandwich. At the same time, he didn't know how to deal with the animals and had yet to learn that saying "No" to them or throwing them outside until he finished his meal would not shatter their psyches. Although he quickly lost any fear he might have had of Shunka, he never did learn to deny the wolf anything.

With the return of Kathy and Shoney, the household was enlarged so that someone was always available to pet, scratch and play with the pups. This constant attention from a number of different people was to have a profound affect on Shunka in that he was never to lose his capacity for welcoming new people into his world, even after he passed the crucial age of twenty weeks—the point at which most wolves no longer accept outsiders. It is, of course, only conjecture that the nonexclusivity of Shunka's human family during his early formative months contributed to his openness as an adult wolf, but nevertheless, Shunka was extraordinary in that he would never cease to enjoy the excitement of making new friends.

Being eager "parents" of a young wolf, we did not wish to fall behind on his education, and, on the third day, the leash walking lessons were resumed. David had hit upon a new plan—a modification of the reinforcement-by-reward method, also known as the carrot-on-the-end-of-a-stick ploy. The question was, what should be used for the carrot? Raw meat excited him too much, and doggy biscuits were not considered by Shunka to be worthy of unnecessary effort. David decided to try raw fish, having once read that fish were part of a wild wolf's diet.

Although one imagines the wolf as an animal who continuously feasts on deer, moose and caribou, and other such large game animals, in reality he must more often than not make do with rodents, rabbits and fish—and, consequently, he is a very clever fisherman. Choosing a shallow pool along the shore of a lake or river, the wolf wades into the deeper water and patiently watches for a tell-tale silver streak along his path. Once catching sight of a likely candidate for dinner, he slowly and patiently herds the fish toward the predetermined shallow pool, where caught between rocks and stones, with one quick swat from the wolf's paw the fish becomes a satisfying meal.

Although Shunka enjoyed exploring and splashing in his water basin, it was doubtful that fish were on his mind. Nevertheless, David bought a fresh trout at the market and dropped it into the water dish. Shunka cautiously crept toward the basin and feigned darting attacks at the fish while Happy sniffed it, stared at it for a moment and then lost interest. It took Shunka a few minutes before he was convinced the unfamiliar object would not attack, and having thus made up his mind, he pounced upon the fish with both front paws, flipping it out of the water and onto the grass. He was still unaware that fish was food, but it didn't matter. It was a trophy and he proudly paraded it around.

An hour later, the fish disappeared, and David and I assumed Shunka had eaten it. Not so, we quickly found out as a shrill scream echoed from the living room. Kathy was staring at the couch, hands cupped across her mouth, her eyes fixed with horror upon a dead trout half protruding from between the cushions. Shunka had claimed the couch as his own domain, and when he was allowed into the living room he frequently stashed certain prize items into the cracks and crevices of the sofa.

The trout was quickly disposed of, but David had a follow-up plan. Along with the trout, he had purchased a large quantity of smelts, and these, being smaller in size, he mixed in with Shunka's next meal. The smelts disappeared down the wolf's throat easily, and David threw in a few extra ones for dessert. The wolf was hooked on fish.

Thus fortified with dog yummies for Happy and smelts for the wolf (a major sacrifice for David since the slightest hint of fish odor made him ill), the walks became twice-daily rituals. The lessons followed a natural progression. At first, Shunka again sat belligerently down on the sidewalk. David continued to walk ahead until the leash became taut and then held out a smelt. Unable to resist the treat, Shunka got up and grabbed the fish, swallowing it in one gulp. This process was repeated again and again and, half an hour later, we had moved the length of one block.

Each time out met with less resistance from Shunka. He no longer sat down the minute David put him on the sidewalk but expectantly awaited the tug on the leash which signified "smelt." Within a matter of days, he trotted along quite amiably, demanding only the occasional smelt as a reward for his agreeable behavior. Always anxious to please, Happy accepted her role with less resistance, her only demand being that she and the person walking her had to be in front of the wolf.

Now that an understanding had been reached between David and Shunka as to the function of the leash, the walks became little adventures which the animals looked forward to. No longer disturbed by the leash, Shunka took an intense interest in the new sights and smells and each time thoroughly checked out every inch of the soon-familiar path. The high point of any walk was, of course, meeting another animal. Unfortunately, in his overwhelming eagerness to make new friends, Shunka frightened off most dogs who approached him.

Shunka's first encounter with a four-footed neighbor—a handsome and dignified black Labrador who regularly patrolled the block—was a total failure. Spotting us from across the street, the proud dog trotted slowly and purposefully toward us, ears erect and tail cautiously wagging as if to question the intentions of the two young creatures prancing along "his" sidewalk on silver chains. Even before the dog reached us, Shunka began squeaking and whimpering, anxiously bowing toward the older dog. The Labrador stopped for a moment to consider this agitated behavior, but his curiosity exceeding his caution, he resolutely approached the wolf and commenced to sniff out the invader's identity. Shunka immediately rolled over on his back and licked and nibbled the black dog's muzzle. The Lab jumped backward on stiff legs, cocked his head quizzically at Shunka and then spun around and ran down the street, his tail between his legs, his eyes crazed as if he had seen an apparition. Not all dogs reacted to Shunka with such extreme alarm, but very few understood his language.

Chapter 5

Every self-respecting wolf should know how to howl, and we began Shunka's lessons almost immediately. Our first attempts met with dismal failure, and we felt foolish as the sound of our hesitant and unsure voices echoed around the dining room. Shunka merely glanced at us and walked out.

Undaunted and far from discouraged, David retrieved the wolf and carried him into the living room, where I had pulled out "The Language and Music of the Wolves" album and put it on the turntable. It was the same record we had tried on Shunka during his first night at Manor Road. This time Shunka didn't walk out, but he didn't howl either. He listened intently as the howls and yaps resounded through the house in quick succession and strained his ears forward as if he were trying to determine the direction and identity of the howls. He paced the room in an obvious state of agitation and, at one point, lifted his nose toward the ceiling in the classical howl position—but no sound came out. The lesson was quickly ended when Happy, bored and irritated over the fuss and attention paid Shunka, attacked the wolf.

On our next try, we mounted an all-out effort and herded everyone into the living room for a communal howl. The same record was again put on the turntable, the volume was turned up, and David and I raised our voices to match the sounds blaring from the speakers. Ian and Kathy joined in, and after a little coaxing, Shoney added one or two sincere yowls to the dissonant chorus. Happy too was caught up in the mood and excitedly bayed and yapped with the group. Only Shunka remained silent and listened, his eyes half closed, his mouth panting. Just as we were ready to give up, he pointed his muzzle toward the ceiling, flattened his ears back against his head and cupping his mouth around his teeth, gave forth a reedy, extended whine. Everyone smiled and, gathering new strength and enthusiasm, answered him with another chorus. Again Shunka howled, this time with a series of high-pitched, yappy yowls. His voice was yet to develop, but he knew how to howl.

After that, we howled together at least once every day, and anyone who happened to be around was asked to join in. Group howling is a happy, social event among wolves and is accompanied by much tail wagging, nuzzling and excitement among the pack members. As is true with any orchestra, each session was preceded by a warm-up. We began the howl, and then Happy joined in. Shunka pranced excitedly from one person to another, licking faces and talking with little throaty moans and gurgles. The tension built in him until he had to give voice to his emotion in song—first testing his vocal chords with a few, short aborted howls until he found his own pitch, separate and distinguishable from everyone else's. With each song session he gained confidence and experimented with a wider range of sound.

The record album was, for the most part, discarded—until one day, sitting alone with Shunka in the living room, I let it play itself out, carefully watching Shunka's reaction to each new howl. As far as I could tell, one wolf sounded pretty much like another, give or take a natural variance in resonance and length of song. Throughout this extended concert, Shunka seemed preoccupied with sniffing the various items on the coffee table, looking to steal a book, cigarette butt or other forbidden item. Suddenly he stopped and listened as a deep mournful howl, beginning in a crescendo and dropping to a low moan, echoed through the room for at least ten seconds. Lifting his head, he answered with an up and down lonesome call, as identical to the melancholy mature howl from the record player as his yet untrained puppy voice would allow, bringing forth in one sad, intense call all the ancient song of his mysterious past. It was the only howl on the record that he would ever respond to, and after that, we used it often to begin our routine songfests.

The August days were warm and sunny, and most of the time with the animals was spent outside. Having familiarized himself with the immediate territory of the back yard, Shunka was eager to explore the rest of the neighborhood—at his own leisure and without the restraint of a leash. We had not previously been faced with this particular problem because Shunka had not shown any interest beyond the imaginary territorial boundary marked by the edge of the asphalt driveway. We had become so confident that neither animal would roam from the yard that we left them unattended for short periods of time—although always keeping the back door open and an eye out the door.

It was, therefore, a shock when, having gone inside to answer the telephone, I came out to find Shunka and Happy had disappeared. Seized by panic, I raced to the front calling out their names—although Happy was the only one of the two that seemed to recognize that she had a name. I was home alone and didn't know in which direction to begin my search. I turned right and began down the long stretch of street lined by brick houses and green lawns, yelling "Happy, Shunka, Happy," when a little black bundle of fur raced gleefully toward me from behind a house.

I tucked Happy under my right arm and continued down the street. Still no sign of Shunka. My search ended three blocks later when I heard the familiar and now-so-welcome whimpering and mouse-like squeaking. Shunka had come upon an elderly collie—nearly blind and taking in the sun on her front porch—and the wolf was busily courting the old dog, appropriately named Duchess. Surprisingly, Duchess tolerated Shunka's fawning and acknowledged the wolf with an occasional jab with her snout, which action sent Shunka into renewed fits of joy and love.

From that day on, it was impossible to keep Shunka confined to the yard. Once he was aware there was a whole other world out there and that no real barrier existed to keep him from exploring that outside world, he insisted on taking off on his own and paying daily visits to Duchess.

Neither David nor I wanted to use the chains on them again and we began an earnest program of teaching Shunka and Happy the limits to their freedom. Our dilemma was compounded by the fact that we did not know how to show Shunka our displeasure at his new antics. A parent wolf might have snapped at the cub's haunches and shaken him hard by the scruff of the neck, but we didn't know how Shunka would react to any form of physical punishment from us—nor were we willing to find out, concerned that such aggressive action might break Shunka's spirit or cause him to withdraw from us.

An indication of Shunka's feelings about physical punishment was made clear when David slapped Happy the next time she wandered. It was David's intention that, in taking Happy to task for her misbehavior—which was usually shared if not altogether inspired by the wolf—Shunka would understand our disapproval. David slapped Happy twice, very lightly on the rump. She cowered and yelped, more at the harsh sound of David's voice than any pain inflicted. Shunka became extremely agitated, whimpered sadly, and tried to drag Happy free of her tormentor. It was obvious that this tactic was not going to work, nor was it fair to Happy.

We next tried our sternest "No" voices, picking up the wolf and vehemently shaking him to drive home the point. Still he darted toward the driveway. In fact, to Shunka it became a game. I stood on the boundary, ready to thwart any escape attempts. Each time Shunka crossed the line, I wildly flailed my arms, stamped my feet, jumped up and down and shouted "No, Shunka, no!" He backed off, but not for long. The moment the driveway was unguarded, Shunka was off and running, Happy in tow, and could usually be found paying his respects to Duchess.

We had no choice but to resort to the chains, something we had not done since Shunka's first day with us. Each time Shunka took off with Happy, David carried them back and hooked them onto the chains staked ten feet apart. Shunka hated the chain and because of his abhorrence of being so ignobly staked out, we hoped he would eventually give up his determination to wander. This strategy was as painful and distasteful for us as it was for Shunka. I could not bear to watch his valiant struggle to free himself, and Happy's shrieks of protest were enough to curdle anyone's blood. I begged David to release them.

Two minutes later, Shunka was in the neighbor's yard, frolicking about as if nothing unpleasant had happened, while Happy longingly watched him from within her now-recognized boundaries. The wolf bounced over to her, bowing and entreating her to again join in the game, but Happy had learned to accept our definition of right and wrong and remained on home ground.

David was set for battle. He grabbed the wolf and vowed that he was to stay on the chain for an hour—and if I couldn't stand it, it would probably be a good idea if I went for a walk until it was over. I stayed—and watched and fretted. Shunka lunged and strained against the chain, rolled and maneuvered, but the clasp held firmly. To make matters worse, Happy was now free, having been a good dog, but instead of commiserating with the wolf's plight, she teased and taunted him, darting at him and then running away just out of his reach. In keeping with our policy of equal treatment, Happy was soon also chained to the stake.

Half an hour later, all was peaceful in the yard. Shunka had resigned himself to his fate and lay on his side, limp and lifeless. He made no move as we approached him, although Happy—as soon as she realized she was noticed—again began to scream like a banshee. The sight of the two of them brought everyone close to tears. Shoney thought we were just a little too harsh with the pups, Kathy was driven out of the house by Happy's cries, and Ian was forced to abandon work on the dog house because he could not stand to work within sight of such abject misery.

A general conference was called, and it was decided that, for the peace of the household, the happiness of the animals and everyone's sanity, we should erect a fence between the house and the garage, thereby closing off Shunka's road to temptation. David bought twenty-five feet of four-foot-high green wire fencing, and he and Shoney erected the barrier that afternoon. The hateful stakes were removed from the ground.

Less than two weeks after Shunka's arrival, Ian completed the dog-wolf house. The structure, which now sat in the driveway, was not only the finest dog house every built, it was also the heaviest. It was practically impossible to move it, much less lift it over the green fence for which we had not bothered to provide a gate. Consequently, the fence had to be temporarily dismantled. Kathy and I picked a nice spot in a corner of the yard, and with much heaving and tugging, Ian, Shoney and David inched the house into place. Kathy picked up Happy and put her inside. I held Shunka in my arms and was about to put him next to Happy when he jumped free from my grasp and scrambled beneath a bush.

David dragged the reluctant wolf out of hiding and set him in front of the miniature house. Shunka would have nothing to do with it. Not even Happy's apparent comfort within the spacious, cool enclosure reassured him. As far as Shunka was concerned, it was a trap—a black hole which held unknown dangers.

Out came the bag of smelts, and David crawled into the dog house, holding out one of the fish to Shunka. Gingerly, Shunka approached the doorway. After much mincing about and many fake lunges at the smelt so temptingly held within his reach, he finally made his move. With one quick dart of his head, he had the smelt and was off to the other side of the yard to devour his catch beyond the shadow of the menacing structure. David took another fish and this time placed it on the floor inside the dog house. I marveled at Shunka's ability to stretch his body as he strained forward to retrieve the morsel laid out for him. As soon as Shunka stuck his head inside the doorway, David grabbed the cub and pulled him into the house, hugging him close and trying to reassure him, explaining to the quaking wolf the merits of this marvelous new home. Shunka squirmed and struggled, and we knew it was hopeless.

The dog house that Ian had so painstakingly built remained in the back yard, a lovely piece of craftsmanship, but empty and useless. It was some time before we were to understand that Shunka's reaction was merely another example of one of his lupine syndromes—the wolf-trap syndrome, which is an instinctual wariness wolves have of being caught or cornered without a second avenue of escape. Shunka was to exhibit this fear and caution all his life.

Since Shunka had rejected the dog house, the animals continued to sleep in the dining room, and David continued to share the floor with dog and wolf. Meanwhile, I began to feel slighted and David was beginning to long for the comfort of a real bed. Since Shunka had seemingly adjusted well to his new home, David decided he could move back upstairs without traumatizing the animals. However, it was not to be. Just as we were drifting off to sleep, a terrible banging and yelping resounded from below. Shunka, egged on by Happy's yowls and yelps, was unrelentingly hurling his little body against the wooden partition and trying to pull himself over the top by the strength of his front paws. Hoping they would wear themselves out and fall asleep, we ignored them and lay in bed wincing as each new assault hit the board. We wondered if anyone in the house would be on speaking terms with us in the morning.

Much to our horror—having failed to break through the wooden barrier—Shunka broke into a long, echoing howl. The lessons had paid off in ways we had not expected. He continued his lament for twenty minutes, by which time our resistance broke and we admitted defeat. David stumbled back downstairs with the sleeping bag.

"Enough," I thought." If you can't beat them, join them." And dragging out my own sleeping bag, I trailed down after David. My stay was short-lived. As I stretched out on the floor, my head was suddenly embraced by the undelicate jaws of an overjoyous wolf, sharp teeth scraping my scalp, and nails from his paws scratching my face and shoulder. Shunka was welcoming me to his den. I was not in good humor and did not accept his welcome graciously. Turtlelike, I drew into the shelter of my sleeping bag, sweating and fuming at the cursed wolf who seemed to have no respect or concern for my exhaustion.

I sighed, and irritatedly wriggled my toes. Happy took this as a signal to add to my torment and, pouncing at my feet, gnawed and chewed at the offending toe through the sleeping bag. Shunka had meanwhile rediscovered me inside the bag and again proceeded to maul my head and pull out strands of hair—being generally playful and still intent on welcoming me to his pack. His welcome, although well meant, was enough to send me hysterically screaming back upstairs in tears, cursing the idiocy of a husband who loved wolves so much that he would endure harassment to a degree which I thought must surely qualify as pure masochism.

Nevertheless, Shunka had won his battle for David; for the rest of our stay at Manor Road, David continued to sleep downstairs while I, chicken-hearted and intolerant of wolfish games at 2 A.M., slept upstairs in the safety of our bedroom.

Even with this arrangement, the nights did not always pass in calm silence. Having discovered howling, Shunka often disturbed the sleeping household with wolf-puppy howls, singing his little heart out in the wee hours of the night—usually accompanied by Happy's shrill yaps. Nothing distracted him from his concert until he had finished his song.

During these songfests, everyone ran around closing doors and windows, praying that the neighbors would not notice the strange sounds emitting from our house. Surprisingly, we never heard any complaints. Perhaps those who heard Shunka were too perplexed at the sound of wolf howls resounding through city streets to report it to anyone lest the reports be dismissed as nighttime hallucinations.

Although most people who met the little wolf cub were completely won over, we soon discovered that not everyone loved Shunka. This fact was brought home with amusing clarity when Homespun came to visit. Homespun was a "cool" wheeler-dealer who was always fashionably attired in boots, beads, leathers and flowing locks. Since he had been a frequent overnight guest at the house (Homespun lived out of town), we wondered why we hadn't seen him since Shunka's arrival. We could hardly believe it was because he was terrified of the wolf, and laughed when he said no one in his right mind would come around our place, what with a wild animal on the loose—and if he could please have the stuff he'd left behind, he would like to be on his way.

I didn't think he was serious and insisted he meet Happy and Shunka. David offered to hold Shunka tightly in his arms to make sure the cub didn't lunge at Homespun. Meanwhile, Shunka and Happy—having heard the sound of a new person on the other side of the kitchen partition—were frantically banging against the board and now and then a little nose peered over the edge. We convinced Homespun to at least look into the kitchen. We were sure once he saw Shunka he would forget his ridiculous fear. Homespun, however, was not to be convinced. He leaned over the partition and glanced at the whimpering dog and wolf on the other side. "Very nice," he said, "but I'd be careful if I were you," and was out the door in three long steps. It was the last time we saw him.

A more serious incident occurred when Mr. and Mrs. Stratten came to visit. They settled down in the living room, and I removed the partition separating Shunka and Happy from the rest of us. The animals came bouncing in, eager and happy to make new acquaintances. As Shunka began sniffing and licking the toe of Mr. Stratten's right shoe, the room became quiet and tense—Mr. Stratten had already made it clear he did not favor wolves. Without warning, a sharp kick sent Shunka flying across the floor. The startled animal yelped and fled to the safety of the back yard, crawling beneath his favorite bush and peering out at David who had followed him out. Nothing could coax him from the security of his hiding place. David was furious, and angrily confronted the complacent man still comfortably stretched out on the couch.

"Why did you do that?" he demanded. "He wasn't going to hurt you. He was only sniffing your shoe."

Mr. Stratten looked at David with disbelief. "That wild animal would have bitten me if I hadn't stopped him," he answered, his voice growing in anger. "I'm not going to sit here and watch while some damn wolf chews up a pair of forty-dollar shoes."

The visit ended abruptly, and we spent the rest of the day vainly trying to bring Shunka out of hiding. The fear a wolf harbors for man—his traditional enemy—runs deep, and this normally insignificant hostile action was enough to estrange Shunka from all of us. In the world of the wolf, man is the predator and wolf the prey. Whether Shunka knew this instinctively, or whether he sensed it by the assertive movements of the people around him, I don't know—the fact remained that he stayed under the bush, refusing dinner, all offers of fish or raw meat and even ignoring Happy's teasing approaches. David slept in the yard that night, hoping that the familiar proximity would reassure Shunka he was not in danger.

The wolf did not make an appearance until the following morning at breakfast time, but he kept his distance from people. He ate only if we left food at the far end of the yard and removed ourselves from the area. If anyone tried to approach him, he quickly scampered back into the depths of the bush. As far as Shunka was concerned, Happy was the only friend he had left in the world, and he followed the unconcerned dog around the yard, beleaguering her for attention and consolation.

I don't know how long Shunka would have continued his alienation from the human world, but an unexpected visit from an old friend from New York resolved the situation. Not having seen Stephen for a long time, our attention was diverted from Shunka in favor of our guest, and thus left alone to work things out for himself, Shunka slowly regained courage at his own pace. Given his wolfish curiosity, it was difficult for him to remain outside when he could hear a strange voice inside the house.

Less than an hour after Stephen's arrival, we were sitting around

Shunka greets friends with wild abandon and a mischievous glint in his eyes. At this age (two months) he took great delight in tearing about the house.

An impromptu howling session in the kitchen with the author.

Sometimes it required a little affectionate wolf-teasing to get Happy (also age two months) to play.

(Photos courtesy David Ostriker)

It was a long way down from the roof of the shed and David broke the fall to encourage Shunka to jump.

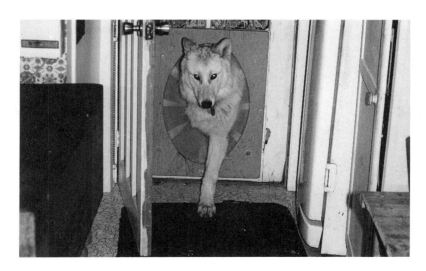

Shunka (age five months) used the Flexport cautiously—he didn't like it, but it was the only way into the house.

Time out for a little affection while Shunka (age six months) playfully nuzzles the author after an exhilarating game of tag.

Shunka jumping to steal Shoney's beret, one of his favorite games, while Happy looks on jealously.

Shunka hams it up with actress and co-star Gay Rowan between "takes" while filming a TV commercial. (Photos courtesy David Ostriker)

A "family portrait."

During the last meeting with Mushka, Shunka (age one year) adopted a classical pose of submission before the dog. Mushka would have none of it. (Photo courtesy David Ostriker)

A tender reunion between David and Shunka during one of our visits to his new home near Ottawa. (Photo courtesy Alar Kivilo)

Shunka enjoying the attention of Rick and Doug Coburn. Children were his favorite human companions.

Shunka and Happy romping in a winter playground at Pickering.

"A wolf, it is said, can hear a cloud pass overhead." Aged two and a half years, Shunka had reached full maturity when this photograph was taken at MacSkimming Natural Science School. (Photo courtesy Peter Blakelok)

the dining room table exchanging stories when Shunka timidly appeared in the doorway. Quietly placing his hand on Stephen's arm, David nodded toward the wolf, indicating to Stephen not to make a move. Everyone froze—everyone, that is, except Happy who couldn't understand why Stephen had stopped petting her. Shunka hesitantly inched his way into the room and toward Stephen who, never having met a wolf, had no idea what was going on. However, he didn't question David's signal and remained motionless as Shunka sniffed his legs and the hand still resting on Happy's head. Having thoroughly checked Stephen over and finding him unthreatening, Shunka turned and calmly left the room.

We then explained to Stephen what had happened, and Shunka's consequent alienation. Stephen, who had immediately fallen in love with the wolf cub, decided to stake himself out on the kitchen floor, playing and cuddling with Happy. It wasn't long before Shunka reappeared in the doorway, ears pointed forward, tail straight out. It was evident he felt left out of the fun and was not going to stand for Happy hogging all the attention. Throwing caution to the winds, he pounced on Stephen with all the wolfish enthusiasm he could muster. Stephen was completely at Shunka's mercy, and loved every minute of it. The wounded pup seemed to forget his grievance, and he and Happy smothered Stephen with affection.

Unwittingly, Stephen had employed a tactic that was to become an important method of relating to Shunka whenever he was wary or felt threatened—which was to meet the wolf on his own level, or even better, below eye level so he could look down on you. In the intricate body language of wolves, this approach signifies submission, or at the very least, nonaggression. In any case, it worked and I was amazed at Shunka's fearless stance toward Stephen sprawled on the kitchen floor when only an hour earlier the wolf had cowered with terror at the approach of any human.

Wendy arrived later in the day—again in shorts and again with bones—and when Shunka unreservedly threw himself upon her, we knew all was back to normal.

To celebrate Stephen's visit, we arranged a barbecue. Now that Shunka was again happy, everyone was happy, and there was a festive mood as all hands pitched in to get the food going. Shunka was fascinated by the flames shooting up from the hibachi, but each time he tried to sniff the bright dancing flame, he was forced back by the heat. Shoney was convinced Shunka would burn himself. Ian was worried Shunka would figure out a way to grab the meat off the hot coals. Between Ian and Shoney, barbecue and wolf were both well guarded.

We talked and played with the animals late into the night, and as the stars and moon appeared in the clear sky and the embers from the coals glowed as if from a campfire, we were inspired to organize an all-out howling session. Sitting in a circle in the grass, we howled and bayed like a pack of wolves while Shunka danced from one person to the next, making throaty talking sounds, licking faces and wagging his tail until he too broke into song.

Considering the close proximity of our neighbors and the late hour, it was perhaps reckless to so indulge ourselves, but it was one of the best howls we had experienced. No one present was left untouched by the sudden sense of primal exaltation, the longing for something lost, and the oneness brought about by the communal howl.

Perhaps David was right. Perhaps, long ago, our ancestors howled like wolves. And, perhaps, now that we no longer recognize the primitive within us, the sound of wolves howling in the darkness of night evokes fear and hatred because it touches too closely upon our own long-forgotten beginnings, unexpectedly shattering our jealously guarded barriers.

Chapter 6

At twelve weeks, Shunka's personality was beginning to surface and as he gained confidence in his new family he became increasingly bolder and more assertive. He was funloving and mischievous. Everything he did, he did with a great deal of energy and exuberance, and it required all our combined efforts to keep him from tearing the house apart.

When the animals were allowed into the living room—which was often, because no one could long withstand the whimpering pleas and unrelenting banging against the barricade—Shunka chewed and tore and stole anything he could fit into his mouth. A tiny rip in the old Salvation Army couch was soon gouged into a gaping hole with half the stuffing removed; the corner of Wendy's coffee table served as a gnawing post for itching gums; and the carpet bore marks of various accidents. For a little while, the second floor became a sanctuary and depository for all valued objects, but this lasted only as long as the staircase remained an overwhelming obstacle of height for the wolf. Once he was able to scale this avenue to an hitherto unexplored world, nothing was safe from his thieving jaws.

His first time up the stairs was a comedy of trial and error, and we foolishly applauded his efforts as an adorable spectacle. Carefully sniffing each step, Shunka climbed laboriously from one to the next, never quite sure whether to use both paws at once or to lead with one. When he reached the landing halfway up the curving stairwell, he turned to look back down to the source of his ascent and realized that, from his point of view, it was a long way down. He dared not proceed further, nor was he sure enough of his ability to come back down. First he placed his two front paws on the step below him, putting himself into a precariously downward-tilting angle. Quickly he retreated back to the wider, curving step and sat huddled in the corner, quietly studying the long descent. His next approach was to lead with his behind but, miscalculating his footing, he slipped and tumbled down two or three steps before regaining his balance. Again he sat down and peered at us from between the balusters, whimpering anxiously at the small group watching him from the living room. I started toward the stairs to retrieve the stranded cub.

"Let him be," David said, quoting the old axiom that what goes up, must come down. Realizing that help was not forthcoming, Shunka again braved the stairs and, front paws leading, negotiated the steps one by one until he reached bottom.

Having now conquered the stairs, he was going up more often than we liked. The enticement offered by such forbidden delights as shoes and kittens drew Shunka repeatedly to the second floor and anyone careless enough to leave a bedroom door open discovered his room ransacked by a curious wolf cub.

Most of the time, the only open door was the door to our room, and this to allow Persephone free access to her kittens. That was not much of a problem. Shunka had only to stick his nose through the doorway once to learn that the room with the kittens was strictly off limits. The old cat proved to be as formidable a barrier as any door and always seemed to be waiting for him on the other side.

After the demolition of one of Ian's work boots, dog and wolf were forever banned from the second floor, and a barrier similar to the wooden panel between kitchen and living room was erected at the foot of the stairs.

Contriving to overcome barriers became a full time occupation for Shunka. Lulled into a false sense of security by the new green fence, we paid little attention to dog and wolf as they played and romped about the yard. I was therefore dumbfounded one afternoon when, totally immersed in conversation with Kathy, I glanced out the living room window and saw what looked like Shunka prancing on the front lawn.

"Kathy, that can't be Shunka," I muttered, heading for the front door. "How could he have gotten out—"

It *was* Shunka, and he had gotten out through a hole which Kathy discovered in the old wooden fence spanning the short distance between the back of the garage and the fence along the back end of the yard. Shunka had learned a new trick. Starting from the back porch, he carefully marked his target. Gathering speed as he tore across the yard, he hurled his body against the weakest point in the fence. It took no more than two or three assaults before the rotten wood gave way and Shunka triumphantly squirmed his way to freedom. David filled the gaps, and Shunka made new ones. Once again, the wolf pup was under constant surveillance.

David and I intensified our search for a new home, preferably a house in the country with enough acreage to erect a proper wolf pen. We spent endless days driving around the countryside desperately looking for a place to rent, while Wendy and Kathy put in time sitting on the back steps amusing Shunka—or chasing him down the driveway. The small yard on Manor Road with its feeble, makeshift enclosure was woefully inadequate to contain a tirelessly energetic wolf. More than half the rotting slats in the old wooden fence had already been boarded over. We figured the green fence would be Shunka's next target.

We had guessed right and almost knew what to expect when the sound of little voices shouting "Here doggy, nice doggy. Come on, you can do it," drifted into the kitchen and sent David running into the yard. There was Shunka, clinging with all four paws to the links of the green fence. The weight of his body had forced the wire mesh precariously close to the ground toward the neighbor's side, where two boys and a little girl were cheering the determined wolf in his efforts to scale the barrier.

David picked Shunka off the fence and put him back on the ground. "Don't call him," he warned the children. "That's teasing him, and he'll try to get out."

"We were just playing, and he started to climb the fence," the older boy protested.

"What's his name?" the little girl interrupted.

"Shunka," David answered absently and, turning back to the boy, asked them to play a little farther away from the fence.

Shunka had developed a strong affinity for children, and that he should have to watch them from behind a barricade was enough to send him into a mild case of frenzy. We would have gladly invited the kids over to play with Shunka, but our neighbor, who was somewhat leery of us, preferred that we didn't.

"Is he a wolf?" the girl again interrupted.

The question came out of left field and caught David by surprise. We worried that as each day passed Shunka was beginning to look more like a wolf and prayed no one would guess the truth before we moved.

"Why do you think he's a wolf?" David asked apprehensively.

"Because we hear him howl sometimes, and my father says he sounds just like a wolf," the girl answered with the voice of one who has access to privileged information.

David assured her Shunka was not a wolf, only part wolf, and felt rotten the rest of the day for having lied to the children and thereby indirectly perpetuating the myth about wolves. Denying Shunka's identity was frustrating, and the next time David was confronted with a similar dilemma, he succumbed to temptation.

It was a cool, rain-washed evening, and David decided to organize an after-dinner stroll with Shunka and Happy, predominantly with the thought of taking them beyond their usual route to the busy shopping avenue a few blocks from the house. Both animals were doing well on their daily walks around the block, and David felt it was time to expose them to something new.

No one else was interested. Shoney, an inveterate film buff who spent his free time writing cast lists on file cards, had discovered some arcane movie on television; Ian was somewhere in the depths of the house fashioning a new piece of jewelry; Kathy merely yawned at the suggestion, and I preferred to stretch out with a book. Taking Shunka beyond familiar territory meant standing for minutes in one spot while he sniffed and snuffed every inch of sidewalk, every blade of grass and every bush along his path. No doubt each of these smells revealed untold mysteries to his keen olfactory sense, but as far as I was concerned, it meant shifting from one foot to another while waiting for Shunka to finish his investigation—all in all, not my idea of a fun walk.

"Why don't you go alone with Shunka?" I suggested.

With their final destination the corner store, David set off with an eager wolf. The first stretch of their journey took them along a well known route and proceeded smoothly—Shunka trotting ahead, stopping now and then to check out important scent posts. Two steps beyond the familiar path, Shunka's steps slowed and became more hesitant. David coaxed and cajoled and bribed the wolf with smelts until inch by painful inch, the two of them arrived at the store.

Shunka was frightened, his body trembling, his eyes bewildered by the lights and cars and noise. David squatted beside him and gently stroked the quivering body, hoping that if he gave Shunka enough time to adjust to the new environment, he would lose his fear and they might continue a little further down the street. He hardly noticed a woman carrying a beribboned miniature poodle approach him.

"What a beautiful animal," she exclaimed. "What kind is it?"

David stood up. "He's got some husky in him," he lied reluctantly, "and I think a bit of wolf."

"Too bad," she commented. "I could have sworn he was Alsatian. They are lovely animals, Alsatians. He certainly looks Alsatian."

"No" David explained patiently, "but it could be possible that long ago, Alsatians were bred from wolves."

She was horrified. "Alsatians are purebred animals. Wolves are, of course, very much like Alsatians."

It was getting to be too much for David and his pride in Shunka. Shunka, meanwhile, was still frightened and did not even notice the poodle squirming in the woman's arms. However, David persisted. "I am afraid you're confused," he said. "Alsatians may have wolf in them. Wolves are *not* bred from Alsatians."

"I don't know. Too bad he isn't purebred."

"If you must know," David retorted, "this animal is as purebred as any animal you will ever see. He is a purebred Mackenzie Valley arctic wolf."

"Oh," she shrugged absently. "I could have sworn he had a bit of Alsatian in him," and turned and walked away.

So much for our concern as to what would happen if Shunka was recognized as a wolf. It was the first of many strange encounters regarding Shunka's wolfness.

I was continually surprised when, after having introduced Shunka to various people, they merely stared blankly and continued to refer to him as a "magnificent dog," "friendly dog," "big dog"—their minds apparently rejecting the fact that he was a wolf. I could only suppose that the psychology behind such thinking had something to do with the notion of a wolf as something other than a friendly and lovable animal. Since Shunka didn't fit the image of the lean and long-fanged Big Bad Wolf, he therefore had to be a dog—or at best, an "Uncle-Tom wolf," which was sort of like a dog. To accept Shunka as he was, meant rejecting the concept of the wolf as evil.

Shunka's identity as a wolf at this point mattered little. With one week left to go on our lease, we would soon be gone—at least, so we hoped. Kathy and Shoney had already moved into a small apartment downtown and Ian had disappeared into parts unknown. We were still looking for a new home and so far had come up with nothing. We experienced a short-lived moment of relief when a woman offered to rent us a farm north of Toronto, but when she discovered we were moving in with a wolf, she changed her mind. The presence of the wolf would turn her neighbor's cow's milk sour, she told us. The subject was not open to discussion, so we thanked her politely and continued our search.

Shunka and Happy were growing fast. The vet had graduated them from milk and Pablum, to Pablum and dog food, to raw hamburger and kibble. The kibble was a necessary addition when both animals continued to suffer from diarrhea long after undergoing the de-worming required by most young animals. We couldn't understand what the problem was, but after a bit of research, Dr. Suzi Francis discovered that in his natural environment, a wolf's diet consists of more than raw meat—the wolf eats every part of his kill, including hair, fur and bits of bone, all this acting as cohesion in the animal's stomach. The kibble did the same for Shunka and Happy. As for the hamburger, Dr. Francis was a strong advocate of raw meat for all growing canines during the first eighteen months of their life, the high protein being essential for proper formation of bones, teeth and healthy fur. The meat was supplemented with a daily dose of a powdered vitamin-mineral additive and a tablespoon of cod liver oil.

Shunka and Happy were undoubtedly growing up healthy, but feeding them was becoming an expensive proposition. They were still puppies but were each consuming a pound of meat a day. We had rejected the possible alternative of chicken heads, which was what Al Oeming fed his adult wolves. Chicken heads were not readily available in large quantities from our butcher, and the thought of Shunka dragging them around the house did not appeal to me. Happy, I am sure, would have disdained them altogether. It was our butcher who saved us from bankruptcy. He put aside all his day-old hamburger for us, froze it in one- to three-pound packages, and sold it for less than half price. If you're going to have a wolf around the house, it pays to be friendly with your butcher.

Even with the addition of kibble into their diet and big green pills hidden in their hamburger, it was almost a week before Shunka's and

Happy's digestion fully recovered and despite David's diligent efforts to keep the yard clean, flies began to gather in swarms.

Inevitably, we were honored by another visit from the health inspector. Two days later, we found a new home—a small bungalow sitting on eight acres of weeds twenty miles east of Toronto in a place called Pickering.

Chapter 7

Other than the fact that we had the freedom to dig wherever we wanted, the Pickering property had little to recommend it as an ideal location for a wolf pen. The eight acres stretched into a long, narrow field overgrown by scrubby plants and weeds which grew waist-high. A few trees clustered possessively around the squat, one-story house. There was not much else to break the flat monotony of the terrain nor to offer shade to a dog and wolf on a hot summer afternoon. Nevertheless, we were grateful to have found a place within commuting distance of the city, and we immediately began work on the wolf pen.

Our first problem was selecting the most agreeable area possible in which to erect the fence. Two beautiful ancient weeping willows graced the front yard, but putting the fence there meant exposing Shunka and Happy to constant traffic noise and possibly other more dangerous harassments. A crab apple tree stood behind the house beside a crumbling tool shed and the skeletal remains of a chicken coop, all of which precluded our setting the pen there. The only other protection from the sun was beneath three poplar trees which stood tall and narrow in a row running diagonally from the back corner of the house. The shade they offered was meager, but since there was nothing else available, the poplars determined the location of the wolf pen.

Construction began immediately, and for a week we struggled with augers, shovels and a rented backhoe. The project was a team effort, and leaving Shunka and Happy under Wendy's watchful eye, we drove out each morning with Shoney, Kathy and a number of other friends to work on the wolf pen. The sun-baked clay soil slowed our progress, but I considered it a blessing in disguise since in the long run it would also make it more difficult for Shunka to tunnel his way to freedom. His antics in the yard at Manor Road had already established his reputation as an escape artist. The seventy-by-a-hundred-foot dimensions of the pen should allow him enough space so that he would not want to dig his way out.

By the time moving day came around, the posts were up and the crossbars firmly in place, but the chain link fence itself had yet to be installed. We were still awaiting delivery, and David's daily calls to the supplier brought no more satisfaction than the vague assurance that "it should be here any day." Fence or no fence, we had to move out of Manor Road.

Within half a day we and all our belongings—including wolf, dog, cat and kittens—were in residence in Pickering. We had divided the animals between the rented truck and our Land Rover for the twenty-mile drive out of the city—Persephone and her litter in the van with David driving and Kathy in attendance; Shunka and Happy with me in the Rover, Wendy in the passenger seat and Shoney in the back to keep Shunka under control and off my lap. Shunka had developed a definite dislike for automobiles, and his passive resignation to the horror of finding himself in such a vehicle had changed during the course of weeks to frenzied, blind panic as he hysterically banged against windows and pushed his face and claws into every small crack between seats or driver and seat.

Despite the ordeal, everything and everyone arrived in one piece.

Before unloading the truck, we staked out Shunka and Happy in front of the house and carried the kittens inside. Persy undertook a careful inspection of the property, and finding the new home to her liking, settled herself on the front stoop and prepared to rule the roost. Shunka and Happy didn't adjust quite as well. If staking them out on chains at Manor Road had proven a failure, now that they were a month older and that much stronger—in both physical capacity and will power— the experience was a catastrophe. Shunka lunged and tugged and pulled and tried to outsmart the chain. Happy resorted to her old trick of winding herself around the stake post and then squealing like a stuck pig. We tried to ignore them, unsuccessfully, and tempers were quick to flare that afternoon from nerves worn thin.

The night brought little relief. We took Shunka and Happy off the chains and brought them inside, bedding them down alone in the kitchen—the room where the wolf could inflict the least amount of damage. David had weaned the pups from his nightly presence in the dining room at Manor Road, and after two nights of whining and howling, they had accepted his absence. Now, however, finding themselves in a strange environment, they demanded that he return to comfort them.

Throughout the night David and I took turns visiting the kitchen, but we were determined not to be conned into the old routine of David sleeping on the floor with the animals. Happy was more unaccepting of the circumstances than Shunka, and she expressed her displeasure loudly all night long. I was sorely tempted to drag the screaming mutt into another room and wallop her until she shut up. But if Shunka was to be spared the rod, then so was Happy. If it had not been for Shunka, she would have been taken to task immediately for her self-indulgent behavior, and we would have heard no more from her. As it was, she did enough screaming for both of them.

In the morning, David again phoned the fencing company. The long, sleepless night had done little for his temper and he was ready to try anything short of murder to get the long-promised fence delivered. Four bales of chain link fence arrived at the house that afternoon.

The following day we held a fence-raising party. Half a dozen friends turned up to give a helping hand; the bales were unrolled and, with the Land Rover being used as a fence-puller, the wolf pen soon began to take shape. Despite the extra help, it was two days of work before the pen was finished—which meant two more days of keeping Happy and Shunka on the stakes.

With all the activity and people running around, both animals increased their efforts to gain freedom. Kathy sat with them for a few hours, but her help was needed elsewhere, and soon after she left them, Happy's yelping turned into a series of blood-curdling shrieks. Work stopped on the fence and everyone stared blankly. "Good grief, what now?" I muttered and ran toward the front of the house, David already ahead of me.

"Wait," Wendy called out, and as we turned, bounding toward us from the far corner of the house with a merry glint in his eye was Shunka, trailing a chain and stake behind him. He had managed to pull the foot-long screw out of the ground and was now excitedly kissing everyone in sight. We didn't know whether to scold him or hug him. Happy was still venting her fury at Shunka's unexpected freedom, and I moved quickly to console the miffed dog. She was not interested in my company and strained against her leash toward the wolf pen. I thought it only fair that she have her minute of glory and unhooked the chain. Happy catapulted herself across the front yard, around the side of the house and tore into Shunka. After she had wrestled him to the ground and growled her displeasure at the unruffled wolf, she turned her attention to the people standing around watching the spectacle.

A five-minute break was declared while everyone played with dog and wolf before they were hooked back on their chains. However, this time—since the screw had proven useless—Shunka was chained to the smaller of the willow trees. It was as if Shunka knew he was no match for the tree, and after testing the chain a few times, he sprawled on the ground dejectedly. Happy continued her chorus of indignation whenever anyone glanced in her direction, but Shunka remained motionless, staring at the world with liquid, pleading eyes.

I formed a plan, and presented it to David. "We have almost enough four-foot fence from Manor Road to put up a temporary play-pen-type yard. All we need is six feet more, which I can pick up at the hardware store."

"What's the point?" David asked. "The pen will be finished tomorrow. Taking time to set up a flimsy wire fence is ridiculous. Besides, it probably won't hold Shunka."

I was not so easily dissuaded. "The animals are miserable and demoralized," I argued. "They are so pitiful no one has the heart to go near them. They have been staked out for three days—they need exercise. Wendy's brother Curtis said he would do it—it will take less than an hour. It'll be worth it."

David relented and Curtis and Shoney strung up the temporary fence in a semicircle against a completed corner of the wolf pen. We put Shunka and Happy inside. Half an hour later, Shunka was out running free. Not quite able to jump the four feet, he had leaned against the fence, forced it towards the ground, and then scrambled over it. Back they went on their chains, and nothing more was said about the temporary enclosure.

The last metal clamp was fastened on the gatepost just before dark the following evening. The wolf pen was ready for its occupants. We stood for a few minutes admiring our work, and then unhooked Shunka and Happy who had become so meek and listless that they barely responded. We led them to the pen, where Shoney, Kathy and Wendy waited expectantly, closed the gate behind us and let them loose. The two of them took off like shots, racing around the pen at full speed, Shunka not even bothering with his usual wolf-like caution of first sniffing the new territory. It was a joy to see them run and stretch themselves, and we watched for at least half an hour before retiring to the house for dinner.

It felt a little strange going to bed that night with Shunka and Happy outside, and David got up several times to reassure himself that the animals were still safe inside the new pen. Having worn themselves out running, Shunka and Happy were already asleep and probably slept through until morning. If they romped around in the middle of the night, we weren't aware of it and enjoyed our first peaceful night in over a month.

Since the dog house had not worked out too well—its sole function now being to provide shade for the animals' food dish—we had to devise something else to serve as a shelter for Shunka and Happy. After some figuring and measuring, David erected an eight-foot-square, four-foot-high plywood shed in the middle of the pen. The sides were hinged so they could be lifted up to air out the den or serve as shade on hot days.

For some reason, Shunka had no fear of the new structure and freely explored the cavernous interior. Possibly the excess room satisfied him that, should he be threatened, he could still maneuver around without becoming cornered.

The roof of the shed became Shunka's lookout and sun deck, although it took a couple of weeks of practice before he was able to jump to the top unassisted. At first David had to lift Shunka and Happy up onto their new platform. He also had to help the wolf back down. Despite his long legs, Shunka was afraid to jump. Mincing from one edge to another, he stretched a paw toward the ground but, unable to make contact with anything solid, withdrew to the safety of the middle of the roof. Happy, on the other hand, tumbled to the ground without a moment's thought. David finally taught Shunka to jump by bending forward beside the shed, his back forming an intermediary platform for the wolf to step on. By week's end, Shunka was jumping off the shed as easily as Happy.

By the end of the following week, he was able to jump the four feet to the roof, executing the leap in one effortless move. Happy, of course, would never be able to jump that high, but she refused to accept the fact that while the wolf could avail himself of the pleasure of sunning on the platform whenever he chose to do so, she had to wait for someone to lift her up. To add insult to injury, even the cat, during her periodic inspections of the wolf pen, easily cleared the distance to the top, daring wolf or dog to reclaim their territory. To remedy this one-sided situation, David built a set of stairs so Happy could climb to the roof of the shed and share the coveted lookout post with Shunka.

Shunka seemed to have outgrown his gangly puppyhood over-night, and although he still had a tendency to fall over his own feet, at four months his movements were beginning to acquire an easy grace-fulness. His body was beginning to fill out and his fur was becoming shaggier. The mousy tail finally looked like a real wolf's tail, although its beauty and elegance would soon be destroyed by Happy's teeth. The only way she could catch the fleet-footed wolf during their games was by lying in wait for him behind one of the poplar trees or Ian's dog house and latching on to his tail as he flew past her. The change in Happy was not so remarkable, although her coat too was growing long and thick and her tail had filled out into a respectable, featherlike plume. Their weight remained fairly equal, but Happy could still upend Shunka by catching him unawares and plowing into his side.

In anticipation of the cold months ahead, I began thinking about insulation for the plywood shelter. Straw, Kathy had advised me, piled to the top of the shed would keep any animal warm throughout the coldest winter nights. It made sense, so on my way home one after-noon from the local shopping plaza, I stopped at the picturesque horse farm across the road and bought two bales of straw.

My attempt at pleasant, friendly conversation with our new neigh-bor—in this instance, a thirteen-year-old girl—met with cool disin-terest. I had always thought young people of that age either had a lot to say, or were painfully shy. This girl's sophisticated boredom threw me but, undaunted by her distant pose, I invited her to visit Shunka and Happy any time. (Having settled into our new home in the country and with the animals now safe within the confines of a proper pen, we no longer kept Shunka's identity a secret. In fact, we leaned to the other extreme and told anyone who happened along that Shunka was a wolf.)

The girl shrugged. "We're not too fussy about wolves," she com-mented. And then, as an afterthought—"Nice fence you've got." It seemed that was as far as the friendship would go, although she did try to talk me into taking a six-week-old puppy before I left.

I backed the car into our driveway and called to David to come out and give me a hand with the unwieldy bales, one of which we stored in the garage. The other we carried into the pen. Shunka met us at the gate but, as David advanced with the strange bundle, he quickly backed away. He carefully circled behind David as we crossed toward the shed, and made sneak attacks on the straw, scampering away whenever the load shifted. Once we were inside the shed, Shunka and Happy joined in the fun, pulling out mouthfuls of straw, tearing and ripping at the bale—delightedly digging into the fresh, soft bedding. When it had all been evenly distributed, the four of us sat in the shed, sinking into the sweet straw and feeling cozy, secure and happy.

As summer edged into fall, we spent long hours outside in the wolf pen, either playing tag with Shunka and Happy, or basking in the sun on top of the shed, or sprawling amid the straw inside the shed. However, playing tag—or stealing, as I called it—was Shunka's favorite pastime. The game was very simple. David or I strolled nonchalantly around the pen, dangling some object such as a towel or hat behind us. The idea was to arouse Shunka's interest in the article, whereupon he would sneak up behind you and try to snatch it out of your hand. To keep the game interesting, it was important to avoid letting Shunka take the trophy too easily. As soon as he grabbed it, the merry chase was on, Shunka leaping ahead with the prize dangling from his mouth, the loser chasing after him in the vague hope of recovering the stolen object before it was ripped to shreds. Unfortunately, Happy made it almost impossible to run after Shunka. Instead of trying to retrieve the contested prize from the wolf, she jumped on the person giving chase, inevitably tripping that person and putting an end to the game.

During one such game, I became fed up with Happy running interference and started out of the pen without giving Shunka a good run. I was halfway to the gate when Shunka grabbed the cuff of my jeans. I stopped in my tracks. A few moments passed, and as I didn't move, he released his grip. I took another step, and he again grabbed my pants. The second time I leaned down and disengaged the material from his jaws, scolding the wolf in my bravest, sternest voice. "No, Shunka, mine, mine." (Past experience had taught us that Shunka reacted more to the words "mine, mine" than he did to the negative "No.")

Two more steps, and I felt the pressure of Shunka's teeth through the denim. At that point I realized it was Shunka's way of telling me not to go—to stay and play a little longer. Nevertheless, I wished he could be a little more subtle in expressing himself and, beginning to feel nervous about his insistence, I yelled for David. As soon as David's figure appeared at the gate, Shunka lost interest in me and bounded off to greet him with a sloppy wolf kiss—ready for a new game of tag. I begged off and composed myself with a cup of tea in the kitchen. I was angry with myself at having let Shunka unnerve me and wondered if one could ever completely overcome ingrained childhood fears. I swore I would try a little harder.

Chapter 8

By early October the final touches on the wolf pen were completed—a cement-filled trench three feet deep encircled the pen and a one-foot wire overhang ran along the top edge of the fence. All these elaborate safeguards were not to protect people from the wolf, but rather to protect the wolf from people. We were aware of instances where captive wolves had escaped and, mistaken for wild wolves, had been slaughtered. We were making sure it wouldn't happen to Shunka. We built the pen so he couldn't jump the fence or dig his way out. We took every precaution possible to avoid his coming to harm from the outside world. It didn't occur to us that even within his own protected environment Shunka was still vulnerable.

Shunka and Happy had enjoyed constant human affection and attention in the city, and we felt it was crucial—particularly for Shunka—that this relationship be continued. Unlike a dog, who has been bred to serve as man's best friend, a wolf has no natural bond of affection with man. Shunka's dependence on us was circumstantial—

his trust and affection were gifts that had to be earned. Happy had a strong basic urge to please us. With Shunka, the situation was reversed—we were the ones who sought his approval. We had begun to understand what Jack London meant when he wrote "when a tame animal loves you, you are flattered; when a wild animal loves you, you are his slave."

In his own way, Shunka had come to love us—we were part of his pack and, as is true in all wolf-pack relationships, day to day social interactions are extremely important. Wolves communicate through a complex series of body movements. We had read about tail positions, ear movements and facial expressions, and we observed Shunka carefully for various signals so we could better understand him. But some things can only be learned by trial and error and, despite our careful observations and premature pride in our understanding of Shunka, we were soon to discover that we really didn't know very much.

The weather was turning foul. It had been raining steadily for almost a week and our visits to the pen were limited to feeding the animals with only a few minutes allotted to back-scratching and quick pats on the head. That Shunka and Happy missed our constant companionship became poignantly clear one afternoon during a particularly heavy downpour. Instead of seeking shelter inside their shed, Shunka and Happy huddled at the gate and gazed steadily at the house. As I stood at the window looking at them, Shunka got up and looked back at me. Although it is true that a wolf's senses are incredibly keen, it seemed to me physically impossible for Shunka to know I was watching him. The pen was almost twenty feet from the house and the kitchen was dark. Nevertheless, he stood there—eyes fixed on me, ears pointed forward, his body straining in anticipation. That did it for me. If we couldn't go outside to play with the animals, they would have to come inside and play with us.

It was then we realized we had made a serious error in choosing the site for the wolf pen. It should have been connected to the house so that whenever we wanted to let the animals inside all we needed to do was open the back door. Now Shunka had to be brought in on a leash. He didn't seem to object as David hooked the chain to his collar, and he and Happy tugged eagerly on their leashes as we headed toward the house. Happy trotted through the open door as if it were something she did several times a day—it was her house and she belonged to it. Shunka had no such proprietary feelings. He hesitated on the steps, sniffed the doorway and cautiously advanced across the threshold. Despite his wolf-like distrust of any new environment, at four months he was still young enough to let his curiosity overcome his caution. He explored the house thoroughly, his long nose covering every inch of the floor. Persephone meanwhile had been eyeing him disdainfully from the comfort of an old easy chair. It took a few minutes for Shunka to notice her, but once he recognized the old cat, the unexpected reunion excited him so much that he wet the rug. Given the circumstances, we ignored the mishap, but we were soon to learn that Shunka could not be housebroken.

However, it took several more little accidents before the truth finally dawned on us. Whenever Shunka was caught in the act, David grabbed the wolf's snout and rubbed his nose in the mess—a useless disciplinary measure, which we later learned doesn't even work with dogs, much less a wolf. We then took him outside and left him there alone—without Happy—to indicate that he had done wrong. Shunka didn't see it that way. Relieving himself was a natural act and if he couldn't get out of the house when the urge struck him, he chose a convenient corner to take care of the matter. Our displeasure was misinterpreted by Shunka to read that he should not get caught in the act—he never connected the punishment with the act itself.

As with housebreaking the wolf, we were equally unsuccessful in teaching him not to steal and chew up books, shoes, ornaments, sofa pillows or anything else that he could fit between his jaws. Happy quickly learned to accept human attitudes of good and bad. She wanted to please us and was satisfied with a pat on the head and a few kind words of approval. Shunka operated within a code solely geared for survival. If he was successful in stealing an object, then the object belonged to him. If you were able to steal it back, then it once again belonged to you. Possession for a wolf is more than nine-tenths of the law—possession is absolute. Good and bad are human value judgments which have no place in his world.

The animals seemed to look forward to their visits in the house and the sight of David approaching the gate with leash in hand caused unrestrained leaps of joy from Shunka and frantic pawing at the fence from Happy. Shunka had developed a pattern of activity during his visits inside which included carefully sniffing every room, searching out the toys we periodically hid for him, and wooing Persy. Once these activities were completed, he became restless—pacing nervously from the kitchen to the living room or hovering at the back door. At this point, David took him out into the pen but within a few minutes a mournful whimper echoed from the direction of the pen, and we brought him back in. This routine was becoming tiresome, and again David and I discussed the need for an extension from house to pen.

The importance of providing a ready exit for Shunka was driven home one night with an urgency that was frightening. David and I had spent the day in the city. It was the first time we had been away from home for such a long period of time. After dinner, we cleared the kitchen, table-tops and low shelves—wolf-proofing, we called it—in preparation for bringing Happy and Shunka inside.

I noticed nothing unusual in Shunka's behavior. He trotted around the house which now had become familiar territory, and spent a few minutes quarreling with Happy over a well-chewed rawhide bone. He soon lost interest in the contest and headed for the back door. "I think Shunka wants out," I said to David who was immersed in the evening paper. "In a few minutes," David answered. "I just brought them inside." As usual, finding the back door closed, Shunka began his pacing. Suddenly, as I passed him on my way to the kitchen, he grabbed the cuff of my jeans with his teeth and pulled. I was not particularly alarmed. Recalling the incident in the wolf pen, I was determined that this time I was not going to panic. Shunka was obviously trying to tell me something.

I knew if we put him out, he would immediately whine to be let back in. His dinner was sitting on the kitchen floor, but he wasn't interested. "Maybe he wants to play," I thought, and picked up the rawhide bone. Making sure Shunka had seen it, I hid it behind my back so he could steal it from me. Instead of grabbing at the bone, he again went for my pants. Shunka did not want to play.

There was a sense of urgency in his manner that had not been present during the incident at the pen. I called David into the dining room and didn't dare move while he disengaged Shunka from my clothing. Without warning, Shunka turned around and grabbed the sleeve of David's shirt, twisting and shaking it with his head. David remained calm and grabbed the wolf's snout, holding it firmly in his grasp. "No, Shunka, no. Mine." The familiar admonishment. Shunka avoided David's eyes and his gaze wandered disinterestedly about the room. David released him and, as if nothing had happened, Shunka ambled off to court Persy in the livingroom.

David sat down on the dining room floor, waiting and watching. Within a few minutes Shunka returned to the room and, seemingly unaware of David's presence, commenced to sniff the rug—slowly working himself closer and closer to David. David remained motionless as Shunka shoved his face between David's back and the wall, sniffing his back pockets and the floor around him. Then without warning Shunka again tore at David's shirt. David disengaged himself and sternly scolded the wolf. I was getting nervous. "Maybe Shunka is tired," I suggested. "Let it go for now and put him outside." My feeble suggestion was ignored. David was determined to see this thing out. He removed his shirt, and stripped to his tee-shirt, leaned back against the wall, ready for Shunka's next move.

He didn't have a long wait. Shunka redoubled his efforts and charged at David with the determination of a bulldog. Deep throaty growls and grumbles accompanied this aggressive activity and soon little holes and rips began to appear in the tee-shirt. His authoritative admonishments having no affect on Shunka, David changed his tactics to passive acceptance, sitting quietly on the floor waiting to see how far the wolf would go. My courage was failing me fast—Shunka had never before been so aggressive in his behavior. Something strange was happening and I struggled against my fear that perhaps Shunka was turning "wild." On the other hand, perhaps it was merely a contest of wills and Shunka was attempting to establish dominance over David. I fleetingly considered the possibility that he was teething. One thing was clear—Shunka was trying to communicate something that we did not understand. Throughout the struggle, David had complete faith that Shunka would not hurt him. He was right—at no time did Shunka raise his hackles or bare his fangs (a definite sign indicating a threat of attack). And despite the fact that the tee-shirt was completely shredded, Shunka had not left so much as a scratch mark on David. The struggle stopped almost as suddenly as it began. Shunka backed off, walked into the kitchen and relieved himself. It was over. David put the leash around his neck and we put both animals outside. We sat in the shed with them for a few minutes, and it was as if nothing had happened. Shunka ambled in an out, played with Happy, and gave each of us affectionate wolf kisses.

David and I stayed up late that night. We pored over wolf books and reconstructed events from the past week searching for a clue to Shunka's extreme behavior. There were no concrete answers, only speculation that despite Shunka's eagerness to visit us in the house, he apparently needed the freedom to exit whenever he felt it was necessary—if only to reassure himself that he wasn't trapped. In any case, we decided to extend the wolf pen to the house. This new area—the small pen—would be separated from the original compound by a gate so we would be able to keep Shunka and Happy away from the back door when we didn't want them in the house. And when we did, we only had to open that gate and the back door, and the animals could come and go as they pleased.

The weather was turning cold and the ground would soon freeze—there was little time to get the posts in and the new fence up. In the interests of speed and wishing to spare ourselves and our friends the torture of erecting another chain link fence, David contracted a fencing company to do the job.

A week later I was awakened by the steady unrelenting roar of a diesel engine coming from the direction of the wolf pen. The men from the fencing company had arrived and the long-awaited extension to the house was going up. David was outside giving the men a hand and calming Shunka, who was terrified by the loud noises.

It was a pleasure to watch someone else struggle with the mechanics of putting up the fence. David and I were in great spirits—a few more days and the last of our problems in physically spending time with Shunka would be solved. Little did we realize our problems were just beginning!

Neither David nor I was home the afternoon the fence was completed. About an hour before David left the house, the men were stretching the overhang wire, working in a corner adjacent to the large pen. Occasionally a tool dropped accidentally into Shunka's pen and David or I retrieved the implement. The workmen were wary of Shunka and refused to enter the pen. During the three days they worked on the fence, David repeatedly explained that Shunka was harmless and was in fact a very affectionate animal. The men were uninterested and remained unconvinced. A nine-year-old girl and her twelve-year-old brother from down the road came to play with Shunka and Happy, but even the reassuring sight of small young children playing with the "Big Bad Wolf" failed to convert them.

Knowing that the workmen mistrusted and despised wolves, we must have been crazy to leave Shunka alone with them. Our rationale was that if the men were afraid of Shunka, they would not go near him. If they had to retrieve any more dropped tools, they would probably run in and out of the pen very quickly. We left the gate unlocked in case any more tools should fall in during our absence. It was the first and last time we left that gate unlocked.

I knew something was wrong as soon as I walked into the house. David sat in the living room, his face pale and stunned, his eyes staring blankly at the wall. "Something has happened to Shunka," he said, barely moving his mouth and not looking at me. My stomach became a tight knot. "Something is wrong," David continued. "He's changed—he's a different animal."

I took the grocery bags into the kitchen and glanced out the window. Happy and Shunka were ambling about the pen—everything seemed normal. I knew David was extremely sensitive to Shunka and wondered if he was overreacting to one of Shunka's moods. I had never really thought about how different our feelings were toward the wolf. Shunka to me was a creature whose well-being had been entrusted to our care and, although he was very special and different from any other animal I had ever known or shared my life with, I loved him as I had loved all the dogs and cats that had been a part of my life at one time or another. For David it was deeper than that. He felt a closeness to Shunka that was almost spiritual. As he saw it, the wolf was an animal perfect in his environment, and the wonder of living with Shunka was to be in touch with nature. The trick was to adjust our life style to that of the wolf. "I love him because he can teach me something about myself," David had once told me. "When we howl at night together it is not man and wolf but two of nature's creatures expressing themselves completely—thanking the sky and wind for being around us—and you can't feel that unless Shunka lets you into his special world."

I walked back into the living room and sat down to listen to David's story, and as I listened I realized that the terrible thing that happened was that Shunka had suddenly shut us out of his special world.

"When I came out of the house I expected to see him at the gate," David explained, "bouncing up and down, full of excitement. Except he wasn't there—I think Happy was there, I can't remember. I opened the gate and went in—he saw me—in fact, he must have been watching me for some time from behind the shed. I approached him and he stepped back. He kept a steady ten yards or more between us— I thought, maybe this is a game, so I chased him and he ran. Then I ran, but Shunka didn't follow—he just kept watching me. I knew then something was wrong. I probably made matters worse by chasing him. I was stupidly insensitive to his signals—human ego. I tried to get close to him to find out if he had been hurt, to see what was wrong—but he kept backing off. I opened the gate to the small pen and slowly backed him into it, closing the gate behind me. If I had him in a small area I thought I might be able to get near him. Except Shunka must have really felt trapped. He hid under the steps and whenever I tried to approach him, he growled and snapped at me—almost as if he had turned on me—no, that's wrong. Shunka would not turn. Wild animals don't turn. They're twisted around until they appear to our eyes to have turned—I was hurt—I came inside and gave up."

David leaned back and rubbed his eyes. "I feel sick," he said. "I wish I could be sick—something has been destroyed—a link—whatever it was, I was the one to break that link—" His voice trailed off and he shrugged helplessly. There was nothing more to say. It all seemed like a bad dream. I went out into the pen and Happy bounced toward me with her usual intense demand for attention. Shunka eyed me suspiciously from a safe distance, and as I approached him he retreated toward the far end of the enclosure. At one point I managed to get within arm's reach of him, but as I reached out to touch him, he darted away from me like a startled wild animal. I saw no signs of physical harm—his movements were quick and sure. The hurt he had suffered was not obvious but, whatever it was, Shunka felt betrayed and was frightened of David and me.

We combed the floor of the pen for clues and found a piece of metal piping near the middle of the pen. We knew it had not been there before. David checked the pen every morning—refilling any holes Shunka dug too close to the fence and picking up scraps of loot the animals dragged out from the house. Slowly, we tried to piece the story together. Shunka's strange behavior had to be connected to the pipe and the pipe had to be connected to the workmen. Either they had heaved the object at the wolf while retrieving a tool, or they had teased him for the fun of it. David called the fencing company, but no one knew anything or admitted to knowing anything. In the long run, it didn't really matter. The damage had been done and Shunka held us responsible. He no longer trusted us and a friendship we had so carefully nurtured for months had been broken by a single thoughtless act.

There was little change in Shunka the following morning. It took two days of wheedling and coaxing before I could approach him and scratch his back. Within a week, however, our friendship had been completely recovered. But I was bottom-wolf-on-the-totem-pole and, as such, no threat to Shunka. He could afford to forgive me. There was no change in his attitude toward David and he continued to avoid him and cringe in fear or flee if David got too close. He still held David directly responsible for his hurt.

We tried to understand Shunka's reasoning. David had been the first one to arrive home that day—and not realizing something had happened, he had playfully chased Shunka. Shunka must have misinterpreted this action as direct aggression and therefore a threat to himself.

Another possible explanation involved the complexities of wolf-pack structure. Assuming that Shunka related to us as his "pack," he must have regarded David as the alpha, or dominant, male, and as such, responsible for the welfare of the other members of the pack. It was David who fed Shunka, handled him on the leash, took care of the burrs in his fur, took him to the vet—in other words, Shunka's life was controlled by David. It was, in fact, apparent from Shunka's behavior toward the various living creatures in our house that he had worked out a social hierarchy—or pecking order—within his substitute pack. David was the leader, Persephone was next, then Shunka, Happy, and, on the bottom, Marika, the "Soft Touch." Sometimes, however, my position was interchangeable with Happy's—if I tried hard enough. David's position remained indisputable and Shunka must have felt that, as the one entrusted with his welfare, David had betrayed him. We ruled out the possibility that Shunka associated David's maleness with the incident. When friends came to visit, he made no distinction between male and female but was equally affectionate with everyone. David was the only one shut out of his world.

The weeks that followed were depressing. Every evening the gate to the large pen and the back door were left open so Shunka and Happy could come and go at will. Happy spent most of her time inside trying to be the family dog. Like Happy, Shunka too enjoyed coming into the house—mostly because of his insatiable curiosity and the possible chance to steal assorted goodies. Unlike Happy, Shunka's moments inside were tense and guarded. He would not enter the house unless David was safely seated in his customary easy chair in the living room, and if he heard David move he quickly fled to the safety of the pen. It was a heartbreaking time for David. He loved the wolf but could not get near enough to touch him. Evenings at the house followed a familiar pattern. We sat in the living room and listened to the click of Shunka's huge paws on the kitchen linoleum. David's body stiffened in anticipation, and soon Shunka's large shaggy head peered around the corner of the dining room doorway. Slowly Shunka advanced into the living room and David carefully leaned toward the wolf. At this first sign of movement from David, Shunka fled the house. I began to feel the problem was insoluble. Finally, unable to stand the constant hurt on David's face, I suggested we give Shunka away. "It's hopeless, isn't it?" David said. I didn't have an answer to that, but we tried to talk about it. Keeping Shunka under the circumstances was painful. Giving him away would be just as painful. As we talked we felt it would also mean deserting a friend when he most needed you—it seemed to us that during those difficult weeks Shunka was as melancholy and unhappy as David. Possibly we were projecting human feelings onto Shunka, but it was true that he had lost the happy glint of mischief from his eyes and now spent long hours at the far end of the pen quietly gazing toward the house. Shunka had changed. He seemed older and more serious—much too serious for a wolf less than six months old. Despite the moments of despair and sense of failure, in the end, we could not give up Shunka. Instead, we decided to try a new tactic—bribery!

If love, patience and solicitude had failed, raw juicy beef turned out to be the key to Shunka's greedy little heart. Every day, David filled a little cellophane bag with meat, and leaning against the shed in Shunka's pen, held a piece of meat out to the wolf. The first few attempts met with failure—Shunka stretched toward David's hand but didn't dare to stretch close enough to take the offered meat. David persisted and slowly Shunka inched closer to David's motionless figure until finally—his neck stretched to its utmost limit and his entire body straining forward—Shunka quickly snatched the meat and fled to safety. The process was repeated again and again, each time David's hand moving imperceptibly closer to his own body. By the third week of the estrangement, Shunka permitted David to rub his flank—as long as David remained seated, made no sudden moves and had a piece of meat to offer. David next placed a piece of meat between his teeth. After some hesitation and a bit of nervous pacing, Shunka gently retrieved it and stood quietly while David scratched his head. It was a small victory. After that, things began to improve every day until Shunka finally approached David without being bribed by meat and granted him an affectionate wolf kiss. He still retreated if David walked toward him—but occasionally he threw himself on his back in a display of submission and enjoyed a good belly scratch.

The entire process with the meat had to be repeated in the small pen and it took longer to get results. Possibly the smaller area represented a trap situation to Shunka, or perhaps he associated the small pen with the pipe incident.

David also used the same method to regain Shunka's confidence in the house. Our kitchen was long and narrow and in order to get from the back door to the rest of the house, one had to walk through a passage flanked by stove and chopping block on one side and two refrigerators and a table on the other. David sat down in the middle of the kitchen passage, holding an enticing piece of meat in his hand. I opened the back door and both animals came charging in. Happy gracefully took her share of meat and trundled past David into the living room. Shunka, however, came to a screeching halt as soon as he came face to face with David and, quickly whirling about, fled the kitchen—but not too far. Torn between his fear and the meat he knew was waiting for him, his eyes peered at David over the back steps. After several false starts, he again charged into the kitchen, grabbed the meat and ran—all this in one unbroken move. Despite his haste, he left no marks on David's hand. As had happened in the large pen, Shunka eventually began to accept meat from David's mouth inside the house.

Within a month a truce had been declared. Although constantly on guard for any sudden or unexpected moves from David, Shunka had come to reaccept their friendship. The careless, joyful abandon of the early relationship was gone forever, but an understanding and mutual respect had developed between the two. Shunka began again to demonstrate his affection toward David and accept affection in return— but it was a conditional arrangement wherein certain rules and prescribed attitudes were understood by each party and had to be observed.

Chapter 9

For a long time after Shunka's alienation, we abandoned any thoughts of taking the animals out for walks—the authority that David would have to exert over Shunka would only further harm the relationship, so we contented ourselves with merry romps in the pen.

By late October the back field was ablaze with strange, colorful weeds and, each day, the temptation to take Shunka and Happy out for an exploration trip grew keener. On a particularly sparkling afternoon, Shoney and Kathy drove out for a visit, and we whiled away a pleasurable hour sitting on top of the shed watching wisps of white clouds scatter across the sky, sensing the smell of adventure in the air which is so much a part of autumn. Kathy suggested we go for a walk with Shunka and Happy. David and I hesitated, but with Shoney around—one of Shunka's favorite people—what could go wrong? The leashes were once again brought out and, amid much fuss and excitement, both animals were hooked up.

We left the pen and headed for the openness of the back field,

David leading the way with Happy, followed by Shunka dragging Shoney. Encouraged by the wolf's positive reaction to the leash, David switched with Shoney and continued the walk with Shunka—who was much more concerned with investigating the new terrain than worrying about who held the other end of his leash. Given the difficulty of maneuvering through tall weeds with chains that tangled and two spirited animals who zigzagged erratically across the field, I was inspired to unleash them and let them run free. David, however, was not similarly inspired. The risk of losing Shunka was too great.

"A wolf by nature is a coward," I argued. "He won't run far—not the first time. Everything is still strange and unfamiliar."

Kathy presented the winning argument. "There are four of us and two of them," she said, "and since Happy really isn't a problem, that only leaves Shunka to look after."

It was settled, and the chains unhooked. Delighted by the new turn of events, Shunka and Happy interlocked front paws and embraced each other before taking off—Shunka running in leaps and bounds trying to see above the tall grass; Happy plowing through like a moose, occasionally bouncing straight up to get a bearing on her surroundings. As I had predicted, they did not wander far.

Encouraged by the success of our first trip, the back-field walk became a daily ritual. There were exciting moments when a fat partridge was flushed from her nest, or a hare jumped in front of us only to disappear quickly again into the thick undergrowth; but even without these extras, seeing Shunka running free was enough to make each excursion an adventure.

As a security measure we carried small cellophane bags of stew-beef tucked into our pockets. When Shunka strayed too far, David took out a well-concealed bag, rattled it and shouted, "Meaties," which caused Shunka to stop dead in his tracks, wheel around and run back to us at full gallop to claim his treat, often jumping high into the air as an expression of his joy. His jumping ability had increased remarkably. With a strong push from his back legs, he could jump twice his own height—or as high as the tip of David's hand outstretched above his head. As the walks progressed we began to notice that Shunka reacted to the rattle of the plastic bag whether or not anyone shouted "meaties." Happy, on the other hand, came running at the word itself, and for a while, we were afraid she was beginning to think that was her name.

Shunka was a natural ham and an excellent camera subject. He was accustomed to being photographed—people always brought cameras when they came to visit and the wolf had been snapped from every conceivable angle. At times I could have sworn he knew when his picture was being taken as he deliberately struck a pose, gazing nobly into the distance or sitting majestically on top of his shed. It was, therefore, natural that David, a cinematographer and motion picture producer by profession, should decide to capture Shunka on film. So, in the last days of October at the tail-end of Indian summer, camera equipment and crew were gathered in our back field to film a public service announcement opposing the wolf bounty. The commercial was a co-production with Marc Stone, a young director, and starred Shunka with Gay Rowan, an actress friend. Our concern that the bulky 16mm film camera sitting on a tripod would frighten Shunka was unfounded. He ignored its presence and, as if on cue, played the first scene beautifully, standing upright on his back legs and greeting Gay with the traditional wolf kiss.

The next shot, a lyrical scene of a girl and a wolf running across an open field, didn't go so smoothly. Suddenly bored with making movies, Shunka took off toward a distant farmhouse. I pulled out a bag of meat from my pocket and waved it over my head, shouting, "Meaties, meaties." The old ploy didn't work, and Shunka kept going. I took off after him, frantically waving the bag and shouting while David watched helplessly. He had just barely regained Shunka's trust following the heartbreaking incidence connected with the construction of the small pen, and he knew if he gave chase now Shunka would retreat farther. It was one of the understood rules of their re-established relationship—no aggressive behavior from David toward Shunka. Running after the wolf would most certainly have been interpreted as aggressive.

Fifteen minutes later, having sufficiently amused himself, Shunka circled back toward me to retrieve the meat. Holding the bag beyond his reach, I ran to where David waited with the crew, Shunka jumping and lunging after me. That he had taken off as he had troubled me. It was the first time he had shown such independence outside the pen, ignoring the signal which had always brought him running. Nevertheless, we decided to finish the scene.

As he watched me run back with Shunka, it occurred to David that the trick for getting the reluctant wolf to run alongside Gay was to give Gay a plastic bag of meat as bait. The plan worked. Although Shunka was quick to grab the beef from Gay's hands, David had the desired sequence on film before the entire pound of raw stew-meat disappeared down the wolf's gullet.

We moved into the small pen for the closing shot—the classical scene of a howling wolf. Shunka had always been very obliging with his songs and it normally took no more than a few encouraging howls from David and me to get him going. Not this time. We sat around with the crew and howled and yowled for almost an hour without any results. Shunka ignored us—sniffing a bush, sitting down, panting, yawning and glancing with contempt and boredom at the half-dozen people surrounding him. We were hoarse and growing impatient. Shunka couldn't have cared less. Finally, if for no other reason than to shut us up, he acquiesced with two, short, indifferent howls, the sound drowned out by human voices. It didn't matter. We had the picture of a howling wolf on film, and the sound could be dubbed in later.

The thirty-second film clip was soon aired on the CBC, and Shunka was on his way to becoming a celebrity. Calls began to come in asking us to "bring the wolf into the studio this afternoon … we'd like to have a shot of him with our guest … we'd like to have him sit beside our host during the show … we'd like to have him romp with some kids on our Saturday morning program.…" And so it went. Our explanation that Shunka didn't like to travel and would react negatively to the lights, cables and other studio paraphernalia made little impression. "He's tame, isn't he?" was the common response. "Well, yes, but he *is* a wolf, and we can't promise that he will sit where you want him to sit or do what you want him to do—more than likely he will quiver and drool from fright and look pathetic." We suggested the studios send their own camera crews to film Shunka on his home ground with whichever guest or host they had in mind. No one followed through on that suggestion—it wasn't quite what they had in mind.

One of the more remarkable requests for Shunka to appear on television was made by the president of a conservation organization. She drove out to Pickering to meet her first real wolf and had her picture taken with Shunka for one of the Toronto papers. Soon after, she called and asked that Shunka appear with her on Elwood Glover's *Luncheon Date,* a daytime talk show broadcast from the dining room of one of Toronto's hotels. Considering Shunka's table manners, it was out of the question—unless they served lettuce for lunch. The woman found David's attitude unreasonable and accused him of not acting in the best interests of wolves. We were unable to convince her that Shunka's well-being was our major concern, and we were in fact acting in the best interests of one particular wolf. Shunka's budding career as a star was cut short before it even began. However, the Wolf League and public pressure succeeded in banning the wolf bounty the following year—even without Shunka's direct participation.

Not long after the weekend of the filming, we had to stop our field trips. Shunka's dash toward the farmhouse had been the first indication that he was developing a taste for freedom. As he grew, so did his desire to roam, and that desire became stronger than his desire for meaties. The rattle of the bag took longer to bring him back to our side, and each day he wandered a little farther.

The first days after we stopped the walks were difficult. Shunka met us each day at the gate expectantly and seemed sad and quizzical when we didn't take him out. We wondered if we had been wrong in giving him a taste of freedom. Had he not experienced those hours of running unleashed through the fields, he would not miss them. But at this point it was a philosophical question. The unhappy fact was that Shunka would have to spend the rest of his days in confinement.

We substituted those hours of freedom with long walks along the road on a leash. A poor substitute, but nevertheless a change from the pen. Afraid that a normal leash would be inadequate to control Shunka, who was already a powerful animal and still growing, David ordered a harness for him. It was a good idea which didn't work in reality. It took half an hour to get him into the contraption and, once harnessed, Shunka stumbled around like a hobbled horse. The harness was too small, and it was the largest one available. David suggested a choke chain. I argued against it, thinking them inhumane. I lost, and choke chains were bought for Shunka and Happy.

Shunka accommodated himself easily to the strange constriction around his neck, learning quickly that pulling and straining against it meant discomfort. Predictably, Happy was less accepting—or I was a poor teacher. The first walks with the new chains were as much a torment for me as they were for the dog, who always seemed to be in a hurry. In her efforts to push ahead at a pace faster than I could keep up with, she forced the chain into a tight noose around her throat and we had to stop continually to loosen the choker. It became a vicious circle. Stopping left us farther behind David and the wolf, an intolerable situation for Happy, and she pulled harder to recover lost ground. The problem was resolved by David, who paced himself so he and Shunka stayed behind Happy.

Being in front during our walk was not one of Shunka's major concerns. He was preoccupied by the cars which passed us on the road, starting suddenly and skittering toward the ditch whenever he heard the sound of an engine approach. We began taking our walks late at night when there was less traffic. When a car approached, David moved Shunka off the road and forced him to sit until the dreaded vehicle had passed. Eventually Shunka accepted cars passing him with no more than a slight quiver and sidestep.

We soon discovered Shunka had another phobia which was more deeply rooted than the fear of passing cars—one that was so basic that we were never able to work him out of it. Our walks normally took us a quarter of a mile down the road to the corner general store, where we circled around and started back. One evening as we neared the corner, Shunka's steps slowed and became more hesitant until he finally stopped and refused to move further. David coaxed and wheedled and tugged on the chain. Shunka dug in with his feet and firmly stood his ground, his eyes growing larger and more yellow with fear as each moment passed.

Happy and I had already made our little circle around a blue Ford parked in front of the store and returned to where David was still battling with Shunka. "Something must be scaring him," I said. "Perhaps he smells another animal in the bush—a raccoon or fox or something."

"I don't think so," David answered, "but it could be." A car sped by on the road and Shunka reared up on his hind legs, pushing against David with his front paws in a fierce attempt to pull himself loose from the chain. For some reason, he was again terrified by cars. Suddenly a thought clicked in my head.

"It must be that parked car in front of the store!" It was the only visible thing that had changed in the landscape since our last walk.

David looked up and glanced toward the Ford. In his preoccupation with Shunka, he hadn't noticed it. Without a word, he turned and started home. Shunka immediately relaxed and trotted beside him as if nothing had happened.

Instead of walking across the front lawn and in the front door as we usually did, David steered Shunka toward the driveway where the second-hand International station wagon which we had just acquired stood in front of the garage. He couldn't get the wolf past the parked car. Not even the meaties which I brought from the kitchen could entice him to move one step closer to the threatening vehicle. After a brief struggle David gave up and, making a wide detour around the International, took Shunka into the house where we fed him a handful of meat to soothe his nerves. Shunka had not been in or near a car since our move to Pickering. We wondered what would happen if we ever had to take him into the city.

As long as there were no cars parked along our route, the walks were generally without incident. As Shunka became more sure of himself, we braved the road on sunny Sunday afternoons and extended the distance to half a mile, ending our journey at a house guarded by Suzi, an elderly Newfoundland dog. These were pleasant afternoons. While David and I sipped iced tea and chatted with Suzi's owners, Shunka and Happy frolicked and teased the aging and sometimes cantankerous Newfoundland. Too preoccupied with his new friend, Shunka never tried to squirm under the small wooden fence which surrounded the property.

On our way home, we stopped in front of a small farm where a six-year-old girl no taller than Shunka ran out to meet us and, after giving the wolf and dog each a hug, accompanied us a short distance along the road.

Just before turning into our own driveway, we passed the horse farm and chose a path which took us close to the fenced corral so Shunka could sniff the horses. Walking by the horses was Shunka's favorite part of the excursion. He was curious about them and submissively fawned on them. The horses, however—like their owners— were not too fussy about the wolf.

The fall rainy season was too soon upon us, and the pen became a slippery sea of mud. Large puddles and miniponds formed in the area in front of the gate where Shunka and Happy had worn away the grass, and retrieving the food dish became a feat of acrobatics.

Maneuvering oneself successfully across the slick, sticky clay was difficult enough—to do so with a dog and wolf jumping all over you and wrapping wet, furry bodies around your legs elevated the simple operation into a major challenge. But then, I seemed to have more trouble than most. Measuring six feet tall, I had always felt it was a long way to the ground and, thus plagued with an unreasonable fear of falling, my sense of balance was precarious, if it existed at all. Somehow, I made it through the season without taking a spill—the worst that happened was getting my feet stuck in the mud and, upon extricating myself from a firmly mired boot, losing it to Shunka, who never missed an opportunity.

Most of the time, I let sure-footed David take care of matters in the pen, although he didn't find the "crossing" much fun either. To eliminate the necessity for doing so, he began leaving the food tray just inside the gate. This practice was soon abandoned. The food was mysteriously disappearing faster than usual, the tray picked clean less than an hour after David set it down.

Since it was not Shunka's nor Happy's habit to devour their food immediately—preferring instead to nibble at it throughout the day— David and I took up positions at the kitchen window and waited. As always, Shunka ate first, carefully picking out the half dozen smelts mixed into the hamburger. After he finished, Happy had a few mouthfuls, leaving the dish almost half-full. Meanwhile, the top railing of the pen was turning into a solid black line, as crows and starlings gathered from miles around. As soon as dog and wolf removed themselves from the vicinity of the food tray, the birds descended en masse. A few minutes later, they departed, leaving behind an empty tray without so much as a trace of food clinging to the gleaming sides. It seems we were feeding a pound and a half of hamburger meat twice daily to the birds—most certainly an expensive handout. The food tray was returned to its original position beside the shed, the presence of dog and wolf, if not completely discouraging the scavengers, at least making it more difficult for them. The birds were discouraged further when Shunka caught one of them by surprise—all that remained of the intruder were a few scattered black feathers.

We continued to let the animals inside, despite the fact that they were always covered in mud and quickly transferred it to everything in the house. It was preferable to standing outside with them in the rain, or sitting for hours in the dark, damp shed. I discovered there was something good to be said for clay mud in that it dries in clumps or turns into a dusty powder, making it easy to remove from couches, tables, walls and carpets. Still, the house seemed to take on a noticeably brownish gray tone.

During a particularly muddy weekend, my family came to visit. Sven had not seen Shunka since that first meeting at the Game Farm, and my mother and sister Livia had yet to meet him. I was disappointed that my father couldn't come. He was more skeptical than most about our raising a wolf in captivity, and I had spent many a long hour on the telephone trying to convince him that we had not completely lost our senses, and wolves really were very nice animals. I consoled myself with the thought that the others would return to Cleveland with favorable impressions of Shunka, which they would pass on to my father.

It was already dark and still pouring rain when their car pulled into the driveway. Impervious to the downpour, Shunka and Happy bounced excitedly at the gate while we unloaded the luggage. They had not been inside that day—I had scrubbed and waxed and polished the entire house so that at least the first impression would be good, knowing while I worked that it was a waste of energy. Two minutes of Shunka inside, and everything would be as it was before.

As soon as everyone had settled into the living room, David opened the back door and Shunka and Happy came charging into the house. My mother, who was sitting on the couch with Sven, grabbed the coffee table and barricaded herself behind it. It was a useless gesture. Shunka singled her out and, jumping up on the couch, smothered my mother with wolf kisses while she sank lower and lower into the sofa. Once he had finished with her and bounded over to Livia, she relaxed and regained her composure. "He is very beautiful," she said, "but you haven't taught him any manners."

It took us the rest of the weekend to explain that Shunka was not a pet in the ordinary sense of the word; that, unlike a dog, a wolf does not look upon you as his master; that he is a spirit unto himself. We were trying to learn from Shunka, not the other way around. By the end of the visit, my mother began to glimpse what we were talking about. She accepted the wolf. It would take her a little longer to accept the fact that we had chosen to live with one.

Livia got off a little easier than my mother as far as Shunka's greeting was concerned. He seemed to sense her aloofness and, after accepting a polite scratch between the ears, he was back on the couch and settled into Sven's lap for the rest of the evening. He had grown so much that he took up most of the sitting space. With his back end parked on top of Sven, his nose stretched toward the other end of the couch, where my mother sat squeezed into a corner.

The tired old couch had become the animals' special domain. They fought and quarreled over it, stuffed bones and other prizes between its cushions and slept on it. Anyone who sat there when Shunka and Happy were in the house, did so at their own risk. On that particular evening, Shunka was feeling very hospitable and didn't mind sharing. He was not feeling quite as convivial the following day, and Livia had the misfortune to be sitting on the couch when Shunka came prancing into the room. There was no way of knowing what inspired Shunka to do anything. His behavior began innocently enough as he jumped up and kissed Livia's face once or twice before stretching himself out beside her. A few minutes later, he stood up and circling once around, sat down on top of her. Livia extricated herself from beneath the wolf and moved further down on the couch, paying little attention to him as she continued her conversation with us. Whatever Shunka had in mind, being ignored was not one of them. Very gently, he grasped her upper right arm between his teeth. Surprisingly, Livia was not alarmed but merely withdrew the limb from Shunka's mouth. Shunka repeated the action, this time applying a little pressure.

"I think he wants you to get off the couch," David finally said.

"Oh, I don't know," Livia shrugged. "There's plenty of room for both of us." Livia had a very no-nonsense approach to life, and letting a wolf—or any animal for that matter—dictate where you should sit was obviously nonsense.

Shunka had a very different view of the matter, and it became a contest of wills. Very slowly, he increased the pressure on her arm and then relaxed his hold for a moment, glancing at her as if to say, "get off my couch," waiting to see whether the message was understood. Each time, the pressure became more noticeable. Compared with Happy, or any other dog, Shunka's control over his jaws was remarkable, and he seemed to know exactly when, where and how much pressure to use to get a desired result. The subtle pressure soon became less subtle and, reluctantly, Livia got off the couch, muttering something about Shunka being spoiled rotten. We couldn't dispute that but, as she herself had just discovered, one doesn't argue with a wolf. One way or another, Shunka definitely had impressed my family.

Chapter 10

S urprise!… Wake up!…" As if from some great distance, David's
voice filtered into my dream. I had been running from some
unknown danger and, finding myself trapped on the roof of a building, I had stretched my arms and was desperately flapping them, poised
for flight—except I couldn't move and it seemed as if a heavy weight
was pressing down against my chest, threatening to suffocate me. Slowly
I turned my head on the pillow and suddenly felt a cold moist nose jab
into my ear. My eyes flew open, and I discovered I was eyeball to
eyeball with Shunka who was stretched out on top of me.

"David! What is Shunka doing on the bed?" I screamed, struggling to extricate myself from the tangle of blankets and wolf.

As soon as I opened my mouth Shunka jumped up and launched
into an elaborate good morning, washing my entire face and grasping
my wrist between his jaws. Happy, who had been quietly curled up on
David's side of the bed, took her cue from Shunka and joined in the
well-meant torment. "Get them out of here!" I yelled, furious at David
and his ill-timed humour.

SHUNKA

David stood by the door, grinning from ear to ear. Shunka and Happy were never allowed into the bedroom, much less on the bed, and I wondered what had possessed him.

"The mud, David, what about the mud," I wailed.

"That's just it. That's part of the surprise. There is no more mud. Everything froze last night and the ground is hard as cement. Look at Shunka and Happy. I brushed them this morning—they haven't been this clean in weeks."

I had to agree on that point. There wasn't a speck of mud on either animal. Happy's coat was shiningly silky, and Shunka was once again a white wolf.

Leaving dog and wolf to wrestle with the thick-piled bedspread, which Shunka violently shook between his teeth as if it were some freshly killed carcass, I stumbled out of the bedroom and into the kitchen. An icy blast of air sent me in quick retreat to the warmth of the bed. "It is freezing out there, David! Turn up the heat. Close the back door. Do something!"

Except there was nothing that could be done. The thermostat was turned all the way up, but it wasn't enough to combat the frosty gale which blew in through the open back door—the door which couldn't be closed without sending Shunka into a tizzy. We had been faced with a similar problem in the summer—except then it had been mosquitoes and flies who invaded through the gaping doorway. Our partial solution had been to install a screen door and cut a hole in it large enough to permit passage for Shunka and Happy. We kept the inside door closed during the bug-infested hour of dusk, and the kitchen light turned off when the door was reopened.

We would have to come up with something more sophisticated than a hole in the door to keep winter outside and save ourselves from bankruptcy at the hands of the fuel company. In response to an advertisement in a canine magazine, we ordered something called a Flexport—an oval piece of plastic with large triangular petals which resembled the aperture of a camera lens. It was designed so that an animal could enter or exit by pushing against the petals, which snapped back together again to keep out the cold.

The Flexport arrived, an old Salvation Army door replaced the screen frame, and the new animal entrance was quickly installed. The difficulty lay in convincing Shunka to use it. Happy was quick to catch on—David had to crawl through the iris only once before she followed his example and shoved her way through. We showered her with praise and rewarded her with a piece of meat. She was so pleased at her accomplishment and the resulting attention, that she spent the next five minutes going in and out, showing off to Shunka who cowered on the back stairs and now and then skeptically poked his nose through the iris.

Nothing, however, would induce him to jump through it. Since he couldn't see what was lying in wait for him on the other side, he wasn't going to take any chances. His way of dealing with the problem was to remove the offending object, and he vehemently set about doing just that. Using his paw, he bent each petal toward him and bit and tore into the plastic. I countered his attack by spraying the Flexport with dog repellent—not a very smart thing to do inasmuch as the strong, acrid fumes forced him to retreat completely.

When the odor had evaporated, we tried again. Out came the meat and after smelling it on the other side of the door, Shunka plunged through—snatching the food from David's hand and turning quickly to retreat back outside. Except now he had a problem. Facing him was the hateful contraption; behind him stood David who blocked his passage to the rest of the house. Shunka hesitated for a moment, and then bolted past David into the dining room where he devoured his catch in peace.

The process was reversed, David now standing outside on the porch with the meat. The bait worked again as Shunka pushed his way through the plastic petals to claim his treat. The routine continued for two hours before Shunka accepted the fact that the Flexport was not a trap. Nevertheless, he was never to trust completely and always stuck his head through first, his eyes peering around to make sure the coast was clear before he jumped.

Shunka's lupine caution reached such extremes that if a shopping bag which had not been previously sitting on top of the refrigerator or table was absent-mindedly left there, he would not pass by until the bag had been removed or until he had convinced himself that the object was benign.

The promise of food was the only thing that could inspire Shunka to forget himself and act in ways which he would normally consider reckless. Someone once wrote that a wolf can hear a cloud pass overhead. If nothing else, Shunka could hear a refrigerator door open a mile away—particularly if it was the refrigerator which contained the frozen hamburger and bones. No matter if he was in the shed or the far corner of the pen, he never missed. As soon as one of us opened that door, Shunka was standing at the gate, impatiently waiting for his dinner—hoping there would be an extra little treat hidden in the hamburger.

My hearing was not nearly so keen, and before the Flexport was installed that gave warning of an approaching wolf, I lost many a meal to Shunka. Unsuspecting of Shunka lurking on the back stairs, I would innocently contemplate the contents of our fridge, wondering what I should cook for dinner or what looked appealing for a snack. Before I knew what was happening, my reverie would be rudely interrupted by the appearance of a wolf who moved so quickly that the roast sitting on a lower shelf or the cheese tucked in a shelf on the door disappeared in a fraction of a second. There was no retrieving food from Shunka, and I soon learned not to eat, or even to open the refrigerator, until the back door was firmly bolted.

From the day we had picked up Happy at the farm, she and Shunka were never separated, and I was not prepared for the heartbreak Shunka would exhibit when David took Happy into the city with him one morning. She was six months old, and it was time to have her spayed. How it would affect her relationship with Shunka we didn't know. We did know we did not want them to mate.

The thought of Shunka fathering a litter had been tempting—puppies with his magnificent bearing and Happy's calm affability would have been wonderful indeed, but there was also the other possibility, not quite so wonderful. The pups might turn out uncontrollable, unpredictable, and vicious—which is often the case with wolf dogs—and the animals would have to be destroyed. There is no explanation for this, only the fact that a large percentage of wolf dogs are dangerously schizophrenic. It is thought that the combining of a wolf's independent nature and hunting instincts with a dog's lack of fear of man plays a major part in producing such neurotic offspring. Although physically very similar, wolves and dogs differ greatly in their psychological makeup. Dogs are companions to man—for thousands of years they have been dependent on us for food and love, for reward and punishment. They hunt for us, fish for us, save lives and carry burdens. They are our servants. Meanwhile, wolves have, during the same period of time, had a price on their heads. To come into contact with man meant death. Survival meant avoidance and distrust of man. Combine these two polarized attitudes, and chances are good you will end up with a badly adjusted animal with dangerously strong predatory instincts.

Despite our elaborate explanations as to why it couldn't be, a number of dog owners continued to pressure us for permission to mate their pets with Shunka. Even if we had agreed, I sometimes wondered how successful such a venture might have been. Under normal circumstances wolves mate for life.

Did Shunka consider Happy his mate? It was hard to tell—Shunka was less than a year old and wolves don't reach sexual maturity until the age of two. To complicate the question further, wolves—unlike dogs—come into season only once a year, if at all. I guess one could say that wolves practice birth control. If it's been a bad year and the food supply is inadequate, only the alpha male and female will produce offspring, tyrannically forbidding other pack members to mate. On the other hand, if game is abundant, or if the pack has been decimated by disease, starvation or hunting, all the females in the pack are mated. But, since the life cycle of a captive wolf is not dictated by unpredictable food supplies, what governs his reproductive cycle? And last of all, if Shunka and Happy were not paired, would Shunka accept any and every bitch put in his pen, or would he prefer to choose? Interesting questions to which we would never know the answers.

One thing was sure. Shunka cared very much about Happy, and when David took her away, he began a sad lament that lasted the rest of the day. I had heard Shunka sing many times, but this song was the well-known, dramatized howl of the lone wolf. Leaping to the top of his shed, he raised his muzzle skyward and sang long and piercingly of his unexpected loss.

I sat beside him and tried my best to console the heartbroken wolf. I fed him goodies and let him into the house. I played tag with him and carried Persy out into the pen. All these activities provided only momentary diversions, and he soon returned to the lookout on top of the shed and resumed his plaintive cry.

It was a relief to see the green International pull into the driveway and David climb out with Happy in his arms. Shunka spotted her immediately and went crazy with joy, jumping up and down against the fence in the small pen, whining and squeaking his happiness. I unhooked the wide gate and David slipped inside with Happy. Shunka sniffed her quizzically, and as if sensing she had been through an ordeal, licked her tenderly and embraced her gently around the neck with his teeth. Still dazed from the anesthesia and looking pretty miserable, Happy was not in the mood for Shunka's solicitous behavior. Baring her fangs, she growled a low, throaty warning and wearily trundled into the house, falling asleep on the couch. Shunka was not to be discouraged. Racing inside after the dog, he climbed up beside her and continued fussing over the tired, limp body.

I was afraid he would unintentionally hurt her and shoved the wolf off the couch. He ignored me completely and was back up in a matter of seconds jabbing his nose at Happy's delicate, clean-shaven belly, carefully licking the scar. She paid little attention to his fussing other than to snap at him when he hit a particularly tender spot.

"I'm taking Shunka outside," David finally said. "Happy should sleep in the house tonight." Shunka, however, had no interest in leaving Happy's side and had to be lured out with the never-failing piece of meat. We had barely settled back in the living room when a mournful howl echoed around the house and into the room. Happy picked up her ears and slowly lifted her head. Then, with a little sigh, she struggled off the couch and stood at the back door, staring at us with silent pleading eyes.

David shook his head. "She's never going to sleep with Shunka howling like that. We may as well put her out too." Not quite convinced that was the solution, I hesitated and briefly considered the possibility of one of us—preferably David—spending the night with them in the shed. The suggestion was vetoed. Happy was taken into the pen where, ignoring Shunka's intricate dance, she headed toward the shed and, digging a soft bed amid the straw, fell into deep slumber. In the morning she was sitting at the gate with Shunka, waiting for David to make his customary appearance with the food tray. It was a remarkably fast recovery, which was fortunate since the following week David and I were driving to New York to spend Thanksgiving with his family, and Shunka and Happy would have to be kenneled.

Finding a kennel willing to take a wolf could have been a problem, but acting on the recommendation of a friend, we found a suitable place on our first try. A few days before our departure, we visited the establishment and met Edna Ferbie, a lovely elderly lady who raised cocker spaniels and ran the animal boarding home with her equally charming brother. The kennels were clean and spacious enough so that Shunka and Happy could be boarded together. Each unit had an outside run, which was important since Shunka's fur had begun to grow in for the winter and the heated inside chamber would have been uncomfortably warm for him. Most important of all, the Ferbies loved animals. That Shunka was a wolf delighted them, and they looked forward to making his acquaintance.

On the morning of our departure, we loaded Shunka and Happy into the car along with their food dish, bones, smelts, hamburger and toys—all the possible comforts of home. We were thankful the kennel was no more than five miles away, the drive being generally unpleasant with Shunka convulsed by his usual hysterics.

Mrs. Ferbie was waiting for us and took us to Happy and Shunka's run—a corner kennel at the end of the row. We put them inside and prepared for a sad departure. Shunka totally ignored us, having been immediately smitten with an elderly Irish setter who occupied the adjacent kennel. Pressing his nose through the wire fence, he fervently licked at the old dog who casually sniffed him but showed no great enthusiasm at Shunka and Happy's arrival. Happy chose to stay near us, and we petted and comforted her as we watched Shunka's attempts to be friends with his new neighbor.

Before leaving, we offered a juicy bone to each animal. Happy delicately took hers into her mouth and then dropped it in front of her, looking up at us with sad brown eyes, knowing we were leaving her behind. Shunka had neither the time nor the temperament for sentimentality. He grabbed his bone, but instead of devouring it in the usual voracious manner, he took it to the fence which separated him from the setter and tried to force it through the wire mesh. He tried every conceivable angle, but the bone was too big. Meanwhile, the setter was unsuccessfully trying to clutch the offering from the other side. Completely frustrated, he gave up and, snapping once at Shunka's nose, disappeared inside. Shunka was upset and hurt, and we left him pacing back and forth along the fence, hoping his friend would reappear.

Four days later we were back. It was almost dark when we arrived at the kennels. All the outside runs were empty, and no one seemed to be around. We strolled toward the end kennel, which like the others, was empty. However, the little door leading to the inside stall was open and as we approached, Shunka stuck his big furry head out and emitted a sound which resembled two tubercular coughs.

"Oh, no! Kennel cough! Shunka's got kennel cough!" I was sure of it. It was a common virus picked up by dogs in kennels and easily passed on. We rushed to the main house and knocked on the back door. No one answered. We tried the front door without success and were almost ready to give up when Mr. Ferbie appeared as if from nowhere and warmly greeted us.

"Why is Shunka coughing?" I asked him. "How long has he been doing it?"

We were walking back toward the kennels. "Coughing?" Mr. Ferbie looked perplexed. "I don't recall him coughing the whole time he was here. Why, he's been just great—ate his food every night. You know, most dogs we get won't eat for the first few nights they're here. Shunka ate his dinner right from the first night—"

By the time we reached Shunka and Happy's kennel, Happy was madly bouncing off the wires demanding to be taken out and petted. Shunka hung back and, lowering his head, gave forth with two more coughs.

"There, that sound," I exclaimed.

"Oh, that—Why, he's trying to bark. At first he used to just sit there with his head cocked to one side listening to all the other dogs carry on—especially around dinner time. Then the other day he lowered his head with his neck stretched out—just like he did now—and tried to imitate them. Only he can't do it as good and it sounds kind of funny—No, there's nothing wrong with him at all. He's just practicing up on his bark."

Not only were we relieved—we were excited. No matter how feeble and ridiculous the sound, Shunka had learned how to bark. Actually it was strange that he had not barked earlier. Barking is as natural to a wolf's vocabulary as howling, except the bark is rarely used and only as a warning to trespassers. But then, in his short lifetime, Shunka had not heard much barking. Happy almost never barked, except on a rare occasion when a stray dog wandered unto our property and moved too close to the pen. Had Happy been more vocal, Shunka might have barked as easily as he howled.

During the next few days at home, he continued to practice his new form of expression. On the third day, we had a long, exhilarating group howl, and after that we never heard Shunka repeat his strange, throaty, cough-like bark again.

The first snow arrived a week after our return. It was a quiet evening. David was reading the paper and I was watching television, which was about all you could do when Shunka was in the house. Happy was curled at David's feet and Shunka was stretched out in the dining room wolf-napping. Looking out into the night, I was amazed to find the world covered in white, with huge blobs of snow still falling from the sky.

This simple, common winter spectacle was reason enough for celebration. As inveterate city-dwellers accustomed to an artificial world where a disembodied voice on the radio tells you when autumn changes to winter and winter to spring, we discovered nature's every mood a source of new wonder and cause for excitement. In time, we might have found these things as commonplace as any wonders a city might offer, and taken for granted the subtle beauties of each season—but it hadn't happened yet, and like eager children we raced outside to catch the falling flakes.

Our quick movement startled Shunka, and he was out the door ahead of us. As careful as Shunka was in every new situation, we wondered if he would be afraid to walk in the snow. His reaction was the exact opposite. Snow was his element, and he joyfully frolicked in it, now and then rearing up on his hind legs like a bear cub and batting and snapping at the snowflakes which tumbled from the sky. Happy joined him and gleefully they rolled around and plowed into soft snow-drifts. The euphoria was catching, and soon the four of us were romping around the small pen, performing a happy dance of jubilation.

One of David's favorite fantasies was to be a sled-dog driver in the Far North—a daydream nurtured by romantic tales with titles such as *Wolf Dog of Alaska, Wolf-Eye the Bad One* and *Silvertail, the Wolf Dog*. While Shunka was not exactly a wolf-dog and a far cry from a sled dog, he was a wolf. Happy made up the dog part, and David had his team. The plan was to harness them to the toboggan and convince them to pull David around the pen. A special leather harness had been made for Shunka and a pretty red one for Happy. The first hour was spent in getting the animals into their harnesses. This task accomplished, David hitched them to the toboggan, with Happy designated as lead dog since she was more inclined to take orders than Shunka.

The team assembled, David stood in front of the puzzled dog and wolf and holding out a smelt, yelled, "Mush, Mush!" Rebelling against the ridiculous position in which he found himself, Shunka sat down on the spot and refused to move, while Happy ineffectually strained toward David. David's next tactic proved even less successful. Pretending to a game of tag, he ran across the pen away from the sled. Momentarily forgetting his situation, Shunka excitedly took off after him—only to be attacked by the toboggan which bumped noisily behind him. In a vain effort to escape the unshakable object, he outdistanced Happy, and consequently dragged the sled over the dog's head. The team ended up a hopeless tangle, and I had to retreat into the house to hide my laughter.

The straps and harnesses were untangled and David prepared himself for another round. Although Shunka was not much at taking orders, he was not stupid. When David again gave the order to "mush" and Happy strained toward his outstretched hand, Shunka not only sat down—he sat down on the toboggan. Poor Happy, who was all heart, pulled and tugged, concentrating all her efforts on reaching David—which was, of course, impossible with Shunka sitting on the sled. Obviously, the wolf was not cut out to be a sled dog, and he was taken off the team.

David continued the experiment with Happy, and for a while it seemed to be working. Oblivious to the toboggan bouncing across the snow behind her and the wolf charging the sled, Happy obediently followed David around the pen.

It all fell apart when David sat down on the sled. On signal, Happy pulled hard for a few feet. "Good dog," David shouted. "Good girl, Happy." Sensing she had accomplished something wonderful, Happy stopped and, turning in her harness to face David, jumped into his lap to receive the praise she felt was her due. No matter now hard David worked to convince her otherwise, Happy felt that for every five feet that she pulled, she deserved to stop for a love-break. Understandably, the dog-team dream was abandoned, and the harnesses were donated to friends who raised huskies.

Chapter 11

David had met Nikki and Tasha at the local shopping plaza. The two huskies were sitting in the back of a station wagon impatiently awaiting their master, when David stopped to admire the dogs. A pleasant-looking man carrying a grocery bag approached the car and introduced himself. He and his wife raised huskies, belonged to a husky club and raced sled dogs. David suggested they bring Nikki and Tasha around to meet the wolf.

The first snow had stayed only a short while, and when it melted it left the pen muddier and muckier than it had ever been. We did not expect Julian and Linda would let their brushed and groomed huskies into that sea of mire. But remarking that "the dogs were washable and a little dirt never hurt anyone," they led the excited, baying pair into the pen. Although Shunka had met a number of other dogs during the course of our afternoon walks, he had never been honored with a visit from other four-legged animals on his home territory.

The four animals clustered together and, amid much sniffing, milling about and tail wagging, dogs and wolf made each other's acquaintance. Shunka pranced eagerly from one husky to the other—

bowing and nuzzling, occasionally testing his authority by grasping each of the dogs gently about the neck. Instead of finding Shunka's behavior strange and frightening, Nikki and Tasha joined in the ritual and rolled over on their backs in a demonstration of submission.

The social preliminaries properly dispensed with, it was time to play. Although much smaller than Shunka in build, the huskies were fast. It was a rare occasion when Shunka had reason to run full out, his normal playful pace being a controlled, easy lope which still left Happy far behind. Now with the huskies close on his heels, he sprang forward into a fast gallop, skidding in the mud as he made a sharp U-turn and doubled back past his pursuers. Poor Happy didn't stand a chance of keeping up and resorted to her old tactic of hiding behind a tree or the shed, waiting for Shunka or one of the huskies to fly by.

By the time the game was over and the players settled down for some quiet hobnobbing beside the shed, they were well muddied and looked alike in coats of khaki brown.

The next visits, of which there were many, occurred under more favorable conditions—winter soon returning with a vengeance and snow again transforming the muddy pen into a soft, white playground.

Shunka so enjoyed the company of Nikki and Tasha that we undertook a reciprocal visit. The Thatcher house was a few minutes' walk from a narrow sandy beach along Lake Ontario, and weighing Shunka's discomfort in the car against the fun he would have on the beach with the huskies, we voted in favor of the short excursion. We parked in the Thatcher driveway and as soon as Nikki and Tasha were leashed, our little group headed for the lake.

The beach was deserted. A few gulls circled in the frozen sky and hunks of ice floated in the dark water, creating a primitive, isolated atmosphere which normally did not exist in a suburban lake-front setting. Shunka and Happy were on extra long ropes on the assumption that the added length would give them more freedom to run. It didn't work, of course, because momentarily unconstrained by the slacked ropes, they took off at full speed only to be tossed off their feet when the cord became taut.

"Should we let them loose?" again became the prevailing question and as we were dragged along the reeds and sand by four ebullient animals, we analyzed the situation. "Nikki will take off as soon as we let him go," Linda called out as she flew by with a husky. "Tasha will come when she's called. Nikki sometimes follows Tasha."

We already knew that Shunka would not obey any command. Happy, however, was dependably obedient—and Shunka sometimes followed Happy. It was also unlikely that Shunka would abandon his new buddies and take off by himself. Therefore, working on the assumption that if at least one of the dogs obeyed a command to return then the others would follow, the leashes came off.

The four animals sprang forward like high-strung thoroughbreds and raced madly along the beach, sand flying and water splashing, as four anxious people stood by and watched.

Our plan worked well—for about five minutes—when, without warning, Nikki veered sharply to the left toward the reeds and open bushland beyond the beach, taking the rest of the pack with him. Linda and Julian screamed at Tasha; David gave chase and yelled at Happy to come back. It was like shouting into the wind—the merry foursome were so caught up in their game that all the frantic whistling and calling went unheeded.

Finally, something in Happy responded to David's angry voice and reluctantly she turned back, head hung low and tail between her legs. Tasha followed her example, although with a somewhat different attitude. Still keeping up a fast pace, she returned under the pretense that it had been her plan all along to first circle away from the shoreline and then complete the orbit beside her mistress. As Linda had predicted, Nikki soon followed, teasing Tasha for so quickly abandoning the chase. Shunka was fast behind him, wondering why everyone had turned around, and the four of them were back on the ropes. All future socializing with the huskies was contained within the safety of the wolf pen.

Shunka was a gracious and hospitable host, and it wasn't long before he had the opportunity to entertain a variety of other dogs and people on a regular basis. In reaction to the anti-wolf bounty commercial, Alexander Ross of the Toronto *Star* contacted us and wrote an article about Shunka for his column. Mail soon began coming into the *Star* office requesting more information about the wolf and asking whether it was possible to visit him. Ross forwarded the letters to us, and we answered most of them. Before we realized how it had happened, Sundays became official Shunka visiting days. It soon became a ritual. We awoke early to make the wolf-worn house presentable, took out the large tea pot and waited for the visitors to arrive—which they always did with their dogs, children and cameras. Shunka never tired of meeting new people, or new dogs, and as one Sunday passed into another these visits soon became the highlight of his week and he paced eagerly at the gate long before anyone arrived.

David and I worked up a little routine to prepare people to meet Shunka. First, everyone was ushered into the small pen where they were briefed on the proper way to meet a wolf—small pointers such as: "Brace yourself and don't be afraid when he jumps up and puts his paws on your shoulders. It is his way of saying 'Hello.' Catch his claws when he jumps. They're sharp and he might accidentally scratch your face. Don't slap him around or wrestle with him. You won't win." And last of all—"Don't forget to pet Happy. She likes to be noticed and loved too."

Once in the large pen, everyone stood around self-consciously, taking pictures and anticipating their turn to be kissed by the wolf. Some were afraid, but concealed it well. One or two chose to remain on the other side of the fence. If there were other dogs present, Shunka ignored the human guests and focused his full attention on the canine visitors. He got along well with all of them, although not all the dogs that were brought out to meet the wolf enjoyed his attentions. A few snapped and growled; a few cowered in a corner, but most of them were game and played with him and shared his bones.

Of the half-dozen or more dogs that Shunka met that winter, only one gave us cause for real concern. He was Sam, a short-legged, scarred and tattered old street dog who arrived one Sunday with his owner and another couple who had brought their husky. Neither David nor I noticed anything unusual during the initial contact and subsequent play and, satisfied that all was well in the wolf pen, we took our guests inside to warm their benumbed hands and feet. The back door was left open.

We were well into our second pot of tea and half way through David's wolf monologue when Shunka came crashing through the Flexport with Happy, Sam and the husky behind him. The four of them charged into the living room and the house was instant bedlam. At first it looked like no more than a very intense wrestling match, with Sam as the bad guy. We quickly realized, however, that Sam was playing for keeps—growling and snapping at the wolf lying prostrate on his back.

The situation became acute when Sam ignored Shunka's show of submissive nonviolence and continued to bully the patient wolf. Shunka, however, refused to be provoked, and realizing that Sam would not accept his truce signal, scrambled to his feet and disappeared back into the pen. Like a dog possessed, Sam took after him and chased the wolf around the pen, barking and snapping his hostile intentions, ignoring his master's commands to cease and desist from such unmannerly behavior. Shunka was handling the situation, and we chose not to intervene until it should become necessary. It was an almost pathetic sight as the short-legged dog pushed himself to the limits of his endurance in a futile effort to corner Shunka, who easily kept ten paces between himself and Sam.

As good-natured as he was, even Shunka had limits to his tolerance and, finally tiring of this ill-tempered cur who would give him no peace, he turned to face his challenger. Whether it was Shunka's silent, no-nonsense, determined stance or the simple fact that he was so much bigger than Sam, the dog stopped in his tracks and, tucking his tail between his legs, quickly backed off. The confrontation between the dog and wolf was settled without even so much as a growl from Shunka.

The novelty of running a miniature weekend zoo began to wear thin, and by the sixth Sunday, I felt our weekends were becoming a circus and I had had enough. "No more open house visits," I declared. David agreed in principle, but nevertheless felt it was his obligation to expose as many people as possible to Shunka. He seemed never to tire of telling the same stories about Shunka Sunday after Sunday—answering questions, dispelling myths and explaining the general habits of wolves. I could soon repeat his stories word for word and felt if I had to sit through one more afternoon of listening to them, I would go out of my mind. In spite of my determination to turn down future unsolicited requests to visit the wolf, I discovered I could not say no to people who seemed to care very much about the animal and his survival as a species. The visits continued until the spring thaw made the pen so muddy that only the foolhardy cared to enter.

Christmas came—a holiday which we always spent with my family in Cleveland—and Shunka and Happy were again boarded at the Ferbies, perhaps for the last time. They had grown so much that the kennel now seemed almost too small to house both of them (boarding them separately was out of the question). A few more months, and they would outgrow the runs completely.

We had been reluctant to leave them behind. Not that it mattered to Shunka and Happy, but it seemed that Christmas was a time when everyone, including cats, dogs and the family wolf, should be allowed to join in the festivities. We were back in three days, bringing with us an assortment of Christmas dinner leftovers for the animals, a Raggedy Ann doll for Shunka, and my brother Sven—who discovered halfway to Toronto that he had left his suitcase sitting at home by the kitchen door and arrived in Pickering with nothing more than the floodlights for a home movie camera which was still sitting inside the suitcase. We later learned that, still wearing his house slippers and with a raincoat covering his pajamas, my father had chased us for a hundred miles. Although the old International was not renowned for its speed, somehow he missed us and turned back when he reached the Pennsylvania border. Sven was unconcerned about the clothes he had left behind—he was upset about the old rabbit fur he had bought for the wolf and was now unable to deliver. The Raggedy Ann doll made up for it. It became one of Shunka's more prized possessions, and he carried it around for days, sometimes sharing it with Happy, sometimes guarding it jealously between his paws—eventually dismembering it piece by piece until the sawdust fell out and nothing remained but a few scattered rags.

Sven returned to Cleveland New Year's Day. It was probably a wise decision after the prank he and David pulled the previous night. We had thrown a party to greet the New Year—a happy event when all the old friends from Manor Road once again gathered together in the same place at the same time. Exactly at the stroke of midnight—amid the wild cheering and sentimental well-wishing—a loud trumpet sounded from the kitchen and Sven's voice reverberated through the house, echoing a blood-curdling, ear-shattering rebel war whoop. As if from nowhere Shunka and Happy came tearing into the room.

Everything became instant chaos as the small but indomitable army of dog and wolf within a matter of minutes ransacked the entire house and mauled everyone present. Shunka wheeled and danced around the room, jumping on everyone, his claws catching on necklaces and tearing stockings and lace blouses. Happy was lovingly pouncing on people sitting on the couch. Beer bottles were knocked over and the wolf quickly lapped up the foaming liquid spilling out onto the floor. The last thing we needed was a drunken wolf in the house—Shunka seemed to have developed a strong liking for beer and argued violently with Wendy as she tried to take the bottle away, slapping his paw on her wrist and trying to fix his teeth around the glass rim. The skirmish was settled when all bottles were beyond reach on the upper bookshelves—by which time Shunka was busily snuffling the ashtrays and, his face contorted with obvious distaste, he chomped a few stale cigarette butts.

The invasion was so unexpected and everything happened so fast, my only thought was to get the cheeses, cold cuts and party sandwiches off the dining room table before Shunka discovered them. I failed. Before I could remove more than two plates, Shunka's head appeared around the door, followed quickly by his body which landed in the middle of the round, oak table. In a fit of fury and without stopping to think, my hand flew up and slapped the preoccupied wolf across his rump. He barely glanced at me and continued his pilferage.

I stomped back into the living room where, still stunned by the unexpected turn of events, people were laughing and chattering animatedly. "Very funny," I glowered at Sven and David. "Now would you please get that damn wolf off the table! Not that it matters since he's already eaten everything."

"Don't be mad," David implored. "Sven and I thought it would be fun if Shunka and Happy could share the party and say hello to everybody. Sort of liven things up—"

Even if I had wanted to, I could not stay angry. Everyone was having a good time, and it was a New Year's Eve which was long remembered.

A day after New Year's, on a Monday morning, David was called for a two-week job in New York and, for the first time, I was left to contend with Shunka and Happy by myself. I felt alone as soon as I left David at his flight gate, overcome by the hollow feeling one experiences upon entering a room normally full of life and finding it barren and silent. The drive home was slow—I was in no hurry. Shadows lurked in corners of the empty house, which suddenly creaked and groaned with strange sounds previously unnoticed. I turned on the radio, listened to the furnace droning—thankful for the consistent, familiar hum. Idly I wondered what I would do if someone tried to break into the house. "Run into the wolf pen," I thought. "No one would follow me there. No one would believe Shunka was a coward—"

I fed my furry friends and prepared for the evening walk. A two-week hiatus might be long enough for Shunka to forget his leash training, so I had promised to keep up the routine. Happy first—but we didn't get far down the road before Shunka's lone howls pierced the cold night air and compelled the dog to edge anxiously back toward the house. I left her in the small pen, screaming her resentment, as I headed out with the wolf, who quietly and obediently walked beside me until something in his brain clicked—"I've got a sucker in tow," the message read, and it took all my strength to keep him from running off, dragging me behind. This walk too was cut short, and I was relieved to have Shunka safely home behind the fence. We would try again tomorrow. After wolf-proofing the house, I let the animals inside and settled down in David's armchair to begin a journal of my days alone with Shunka and Happy.

The notes came in handy. When David got home, his first question was "How were the animals? Did they give you any trouble?" I handed him the log. "Read this. It'll give you a pretty good idea how impossible Shunka can get when you're not around." I didn't want to tell him I almost lost the wolf, nor could I explain the misgivings I had felt about keeping him. It would be easier, I thought, if I gave him the journal. David sat down and read.

Tuesday: Awoke at eleven—stiff and tired. Fed the beasts and spent the day writing film presentation, stopping long enough for a short game of tag in the pen. The cold soon forced me back inside. Fed them again in the evening—and time for the walk. Tried the double leash, which was impossible. A tangled mess as each animal pulled in a direction opposite from the other. I didn't get more than six feet from the house. Unhooked them and walked them individually, this time Shunka first. Stupidly, I left with him by the front door while Happy was still in the house. She dashed out and I had to drag Shunka into the small pen while I chased Happy back inside. Finally set off again with Shunka, and ran into a new problem. A stray dog threatened to attack the wolf, and now of all times, Shunka wanted to stand his ground and fight. It took all my strength to drag him home—knees trembling and hands shaking. Relaxed for a minute and then a short turn with Happy. I was glad to turn homeward when Shunka's howl pierced the air and tugged at Happy. Settled down to reading, and running after Shunka, retrieving his stolen goods. He is almost impossible in the house. Twice I threw him out—only to relent a few minutes later.

Wednesday: A gray day as I shuffled around the kitchen and made myself pancakes before feeding my animal friends. Light snowfall in early afternoon became a near blizzard by evening. Decided to forego tonight's walk—road icy and footing unsteady. Shunka and Happy are tearing in and out. Gave them a bone earlier to settle them down—the peace was short-lived. It is a lonely night, but my spirits are good. After parting with two more bones, I threw Shunka and Happy outside. Shunka has become uncontrollable—into everything and I am too tired to fight with him. Casualties for tonight—2 dishcloths, 1 carton, 2 pot holders, the pepper shaker, and almost my glasses.

Thursday: Not much time spent with Shunka and Happy today. Fed them and gathered myself together for drive into city. Before leaving, gave the animals meaty bones. Shunka took his with his usual enthusiasm, but then laid it down and whimpered—he didn't want me to go. They both seemed lonely. Having to leave them thus made me sad and confused as to the justification for keeping a vital, self-sufficient animal as a "pet." Snowed heavily and I stayed overnight with Kathy and Shoney. Sleep came slowly—sense of guilt about Shunka, and Happy. In attempting to keep them equal, we have lost a part of each. Happy is violently jealous and therefore unmanageable—her demands for affection exhaustive. Shunka, on the other hand, cares deeply only for Happy and although his heart is full of boundless love, he seems to find it difficult to direct it toward any one person on a constant basis.

Friday: Pleasant morning with Kathy in the city, and now at 1:30 A.M., having finished a howl with Shunka, I am moved deeply and feel helpless for him. I played the wolf record and he went outside and howled his heart out—answering each call on the album—if only there were real wolves waiting to greet him. He must have felt an unknown longing for the free wilderness and kinship he never knew with other wolves. Instead, there is Happy—annoyed and annoying as she continues to harass him at every howl.

A certain aloofness about him tonight—and he is back into nipping me when I'm in the pen. Mostly at my boots, sneaking up from behind. They must have felt abandoned because I was gone all day yesterday and stayed overnight, and then I didn't let them inside until after midnight. At first Shunka was skitterish, carefully checking out the floor and sniffing the air. I think if he isn't inside for some time each day, he has to test everything all over again.

Saturday: Fight with Shunka, who has become extremely restless and troublesome—but there is little release for his natural energies and curiosities. This is the time he should be out learning to hunt. I gave them both goody bags filled with meat and fish to rip open and devour, but it was a meager triumph. Shunka amused himself by pulling out records from the bookshelf, extracting them carefully with his teeth, one by one, and then taking them outside for mangling. "No, Shunka, mine, mine," I yelled, jumping up from the chair and pushing him away from the collection. He ignored me totally and pulled out another one; I took it away, and he made a new selection. I grabbed his snout and gently slapped it with my fingers, scolding in my deepest, sternest voice. As soon as I released my hold he reached toward the shelf with renewed determination. I slapped his nose harder. Momentarily surprised, he jerked his head up and sat back on his haunches. Then studying me with a look of unmistakable belligerence, he raised his right paw and slapped me back, his sharp claws raking down the length of my arm. I blinked at him in disbelief as he calmly resumed his record theft. I felt as if I had regressed to being ten years old, goaded into a fight with one of my siblings. Their stay indoors was, needless to say, short-lived.

Monday: Wendy out to visit and brought new toys for Shunka and Happy, which were carried outside and forgotten immediately. Same thing with anything Shunka steals—it gets dragged outside and forgotten. They are both spoiled rotten. Toys bore them; furries bore them; their food bores them; doggy biscuits bore them; even bones bore them. I think I will cut them off for a while.

Wednesday: I am still shaking as I write this, and can hardly believe Shunka is safely back in his pen. We took our first evening walk in a week—the weather has been bad and the roads icy. I should have known better—should have known Shunka was beyond my control, and that he knew it. As soon as we got on the road, he quickened his pace, and I had trouble keeping up with him. (Shunka never walks but prances with a spring-like, mincing gait or trots like a horse.) He seemed oblivious to the choke chain tight against his throat, even as I felt the chain tighten painfully around my hand. I realized I would not be able to hold him much longer and began to steer him homeward. Shunka had other ideas and, with a quick lunge forward, tore the chain from my hands and headed across a nearby pasture. It was dark and I could barely distinguish his white figure loping gracefully across the snow. All I could think about was "don't lose him—keep him in sight. If you don't, he will be gone forever."

He took me across pasture and field, over fences and through bushes—playfully teasing, stopping once or twice to allow me within arms reach before taking off again. As I ran, images flashed through my mind. He would be run over by a car. A farmer would shoot him. He would get lost and starve to death. Fear and panic kept me on my feet and running throughout the desperate two-hour chase, but it was Happy who finally brought him home. Fortunately, Shunka had been running in arcs and circles—always staying within sight of home. Happy was shut up inside, and as we ran across our own back field, I turned toward the house and let the dog out into the pen—leaving her locked behind the gate as I continued to pursue the wolf. As I had hoped, Happy mounted a loud campaign of protest at being excluded from the game, and her loud shrieks brought Shunka galloping to the pen to investigate the cause of Happy's plight. He bowed and pranced and whimpered at her through the fence, and I quickly plucked up the chain which dangled from his neck. Within seconds he was safely inside the pen.

Leaning back against the gate, I clutched my sides and tried to catch my breath, stop myself from shaking—finally sinking down into the snow and sitting there, hugging Shunka for dear life. "I love you," I mumbled as I clutched his fur, "but tonight I wish I had never heard the word 'wolf.'"

David finished reading, and for a long time said nothing, gazing thoughtfully out the window. I knew what he was thinking, but I didn't want to hear it when he turned toward me and asked, "Do you think we should give Shunka away? We could look for a new home for him, starting tomorrow—"

I did not want to give up Shunka. At the same time, if the situation again presented itself where I would be forced to stay alone with the animals for a long period of time—which was likely—I knew I would resent it. The question seemed unfair. I did not want to be the one to make the decision—or bear the consequences of such a decision. The discussion was dropped, for the time being.

Chapter 12

With David home again, order was restored in the wolf pen and life returned to a normal, manageable routine. The unhappy shadow of the previous days had disappeared completely when one morning we awoke to the sound of tiny squeaks emitting from our closet. Persy had given birth to another litter, and the proud mother purred loudly with contentment as we admired her new brood of six white kittens.

The father, a handsome, long-haired gray whom we dubbed Freddy, was a barn cat and resident mouser at the horse farm across the road—and he smelled like one. He was, however, a "gentleman mouser," preferring to beg for his dinner rather than catch it, and soon after Persephone had enticed him to our house, he became a regular—arriving at dinner time, eating his fill, taking a long snooze and, as evening drew near, disappearing into the night.

Because of Freddy's nocturnal roamings and the fact that we normally didn't let Shunka and Happy into the house until evening, a few months passed before Shunka had an opportunity to make the gentleman cat's acquaintance. From Shunka's point of view the meeting was a total failure.

Perhaps Freddy had had a rough night at the barn, or he was merely reluctant to leave the warmth of the overstuffed armchair. But, whatever the reason, he overslept one evening and was startled out of his catnap by a wolf bouncing toward the chair and suddenly looming large above him. He awoke hissing and spitting and scrambled to the top of the chair. It looked as if Shunka had the cat cornered; but Freddy was no coward and, with one flying leap, cleared Shunka's head and was home free. We didn't expect to see him again, but the following Monday found him curled up on the arm of Shunka's couch, dozing cautiously with one eye open. The wolf's head soon appeared around the corner of the living room doorway. Freddy stood his ground and when Shunka began whimpering and affectionately jabbed his long, rubbery nose toward the cat, claws flew out and drew blood. Shunka backed away, rubbing his injured nose between his paws while Freddy retreated to the top of the china cabinet, which thereafter became his permanent perch. The relationship thus ended before it began.

Freddy's rejection did not crush Shunka too badly. Persy was still the feline love of his life and, now that she was a mother again, her disposition mellowed and she became more tolerant of the wolf, permitting him to lick the top of her head more often than usual.

Elated by this unexpected acknowledgment of his affections, Shunka felt obliged to show his gratitude. Charging into the house one afternoon, without warning he disgorged a pound of partially digested fresh meat on the floor in front of the cat. Delighted at his "gift," he danced around her and with his nose gently pushed Persy toward the mess on the floor. Persy sniffed disdainfully, sneezed twice and, with her tail twitching in disgust, retreated to the door of the study where her kittens were now in residence. I let her into the room and closed the door behind her, leaving Shunka standing at the threshold hurt and bewildered at this new rejection. I was not particularly delighted at his offering myself, but he looked so dejected that I not only forgave him, but spent the next ten minutes scratching his back and telling him what a wonderful wolf he was.

David viewed the incident clinically and looked at it as another interesting manifestation of Shunka's lupine approach to life. As mentioned earlier, wolves feed denning mothers, and pups too young to join the hunt, by carrying large quantities of semidigested food in their stomach back to the den site, where they easily disgorge large chunks of still fresh meat for the benefit of those who have not yet had dinner. I don't know what inspired Shunka to thus favor Persy—I doubted he was aware that she was a denning mother and, if he was, it did not seem likely that the fact would be his motivation. Shunka was still in the adolescent stage and had never been trained in the methods of pack survival. But, then, anything was possible.

A week later, the kittens were climbing and scampering around the house, and David decided to introduce one to Shunka—thinking, vaguely, that if the initial meeting went well, we would keep one of the kittens and raise it with the wolf. Picking out an aggressive, fat little male with a gray spot on his white head, David settled into his armchair. "Okay," he called to me, "you can let Shunka inside." As the wolf bounced into the living room, David quietly held the mewling creature in his hands and waited for Shunka to move closer to sniff it. However, Shunka mistook the furry thing for a new stuffed toy and quickly snatched it into his mouth, wheeling around to head for the back door.

A feeling of sick horror engulfed me as I watched the front half of the kitten disappear into the wolf's mouth. A mad scramble followed as David sprang from his chair after the wolf, yelling "drop it, Shunka, drop it," and I ran toward the kitchen to block his exit. Suddenly, as if he had been startled, Shunka jumped backward and opened his jaws wide, dropping the kitten. The white bundle of fur hit the floor with a soft thud, and then sat there weaving unsteadily and blinking its eyes.

Fearing the worst, I picked up the damp, stunned animal and closely inspected every part of its body. His tremulous little meows were reassuring and we took him back to his mother—abandoning forever the idea of raising one of the litter with Shunka. This time we had been lucky—the kitten's unexpected squirming against his tongue had evidently scared the wits out of Shunka. Next time it might not work out that way. In the course of the following weeks, we managed to find homes for all of Persy's brood. The deluge of Sunday visitors turned out to have unexpected dividends.

One of Shunka's more interesting visitors was Tuffy, a young female brush wolf. Her owner, who lived some one hundred miles north of us, had read about Shunka in Alexander Ross's column and wrote to us about arranging a visit between the two wolves. We were excited about the prospect, and wondered how Shunka would react. Would he know that Tuffy was a wolf? Would they fall in love? Would meeting her make him lonely for a life he never had with his own kind?

After extensive correspondence and comparing of notes, Tuffy finally came to visit. We knew she would be much smaller than Shunka, having been told she was a Mexican brush wolf, which was one of the smallest of the species *Canis lupus*. It would be an interesting comparison, Shunka belonging to the largest of the species, the tundra wolves. We were not prepared, however, for the tiny, scruffy, sad-looking animal that arrived at our doorstep, dragged into the house on the end of a heavy-duty chain leash. She was nervous and tense, and I guessed the long drive in the car probably had something to do with her state of mind, despite her owner's claim that Tuffy enjoyed traveling. He also assured us that she was completely harmless, having been defanged while still a whelp. She had been bought from a pet shop in Michigan, and the dealer had recommended the defanging "for the safety of the owner and his family." We were appalled at the story, and reassured our guest that, although Shunka was not defanged, he would attack with nothing stronger than love.

Dragging a reluctant and whimpering Tuffy, we proceeded to the pen. Shunka immediately spied the little wolf cringing between her master's legs and began his springing dance at the gate while David fiddled with the cold-stiffened lock. The gate swung open and Tuffy was taken inside, whereupon Shunka eagerly sniffed her and tried to place his paws on her shoulders in greeting. She recoiled from him, crouched low and pulled her tail down far between her legs. Happy tried teasing her into a game of tag, but Tuffy remained huddled near the fence, throwing herself on her back whenever Shunka approached. It was obvious that she was showing active submission toward the larger, more powerful wolf, but instead of appeasing Shunka, her complete lack of self-assurance pushed him into greater acts of aggression. Not satisfied at her prostrate display of subordination, he grabbed and nipped at her ruff, relaxing his hold only when she responded with a short, high-pitched yelp. Even if this was common practice among wolves in establishing a pecking order, it was clear that Tuffy was not enjoying the visit. We put her into the small pen where she remained motionless, the heavy chain still around her neck—a pitiable sight as she cowered in a corner while the rest of us played with Shunka and Happy. It is a tragic thing to see a wild animal whose spirit has been so completely broken. Fortunately, the temperature was well below freezing and the cold weather cut the visit short. It was one of the most unpleasant Sunday afternoons we had spent in a long time.

There was a lot of ice during that winter. The weather was strange and unpredictable. A heavy snowfall often turned into freezing rain and coated the world with a hard layer of ice. There were days when the pen resembled a skating rink and not even Shunka and Happy could keep their footing as they slipped and sprawled their way from shed to gate. Other mornings the gate froze completely and, despite David's persistent hacking, we couldn't get inside to feed the animals and had to resort to heaving chunks of hamburger over the fence.

Nevertheless, winter was Shunka's season. His coat had filled out and he looked magnificent. Watching him romp in the snow in all his glory, David and I felt sick at heart that he was a captive animal, and wished with all our souls that we could give him his freedom. But that was, of course, impossible. He was incapable of surviving in the wilderness that had borne him.

As the winter wore on, and our money wore out, living in Pickering with a wolf became increasingly more complicated. David was accepting jobs that kept him away from home for days, sometimes weeks, at a stretch, and I was again left alone to deal with the animals. Then, in late February when I was offered a two-month job with an advertising company in the city, everything came to a head. David had already accepted a six-week shoot on a feature in New York. One of us would have to turn down work and stay with the animals, Shunka needed constant handling and affection to maintain his socialization with human beings. Two days after I turned down my offer, David's film fell through. I called the advertising company back. The job was still open, and I took it.

A major confrontation had been sidestepped, but the question of keeping Shunka once again hung heavily in the air. As the weeks passed, the problem became more acute, more unavoidable. Both of us spent a large part of our time in the city, and bad weather added to our troubles—forcing us at times to stay overnight in Toronto; other times snowing us in at Pickering. The animals were fed and looked after, but the business of daily living was encroaching upon the free hours we used to have to play with them. We began to notice a certain aloofness in Shunka and knew it was because we were away too much of the time.

The final blow came in early spring. A new airport was scheduled for the Pickering area, and the property we were renting was sold to a developer. The final decision regarding Shunka's future had to be made quickly. Neither of us wanted to be the first to say it, but we both knew we could no longer afford to keep Shunka. After three long nights of discussion, tears and wavering, the verdict was reached—the time had come to find a new home for the wolf, for his sake as well as our own.

We hardly knew where to begin, where to look. The one thing about which we felt strongly was that Shunka's next home would have to be permanent. Consequently, we turned down all offers from individuals and families who, like ourselves, wanted the experience of having a wolf in the family. No matter how good the intentions, the demands and responsibility of raising a wolf, or any wild animal, are such that there will come a time when one can no longer cope—not unless one is willing to devote one's life to the animal. And that is asking a lot.

We contacted game farms and some of the new, progressive zoos. They turned us down. In desperation, David called Bill Mason who had filmed Death of a Legend for the Canadian Film Board. He had hand-raised a small pack of wolves to make the film, and perhaps he wouldn't mind another one. His wife Betty answered the phone. Bill was away filming somewhere in the North. "I'm calling because I understand you and your husband own some wolves—" David began hesitantly.

"I'm sorry," she quickly interrupted, "if you're looking for a wolf, we can't help you. We don't have them anymore."

"That's not exactly why I'm calling. In fact, we have a wolf and we were hoping you could take him. You see, the problem is that, like your husband, I'm also a cameraman and as you probably know from your own experience, I travel quite a bit—which means my wife has to stay at home with the wolf—"

Mrs. Mason burst out laughing. "You don't have to say any more. I know exactly what she is going through. Give me your name and address, and I will do everything possible to help you find a home for that wolf."

She was true to her word. Two weeks later she sent us a postcard: "There is a large, outdoor school near us—The MacSkimming Natural Science School. I talked to them about your wolf. They are very interested and are waiting to hear from you...."

We called the school immediately and spoke to Neil Craig, one of the staff members. He promised to drive down within the next month to visit us and meet Shunka. He did so three weeks later, arriving on a clear, sunny weekend with his wife, Susanne, and Al, another of the school's staff.

Neil was quiet and soft-spoken and seemed to have a deep interest in wolves. He had read a great deal about them, and although some of his information was sketchy and off-base, his feeling for the animal was intelligent and perceptive. It was Neil who was keen on the idea of bringing Shunka to MacSkimming, and he needed only to meet Shunka once to settle his mind on the matter.

Al was more skeptical. He was willing to listen and agreed to a visit with Shunka, but he had to be convinced that the wolf really was affectionate, gentle and nonviolent. The first half hour of their visit was spent in conversation. Al had many questions about Shunka and his nature, and although David's answers seemed to satisfy him, he had difficulty believing that Shunka was as loving as we painted him. "He might be as you say he is," he said, shaking his head, "but then he may be that way with you, because you are his master. If we take him away, he might act differently, which is what happens to many dogs." Despite David's repeated suggestions that we go out to the wolf pen to meet Shunka, or let the wolf inside, Al procrastinated and preferred to deal with the question academically. There was nothing left but to open the back door and let Shunka inside, whether Al was ready or not. Oddly enough, out of all the people in the room, Shunka singled out Al as the object of his attention. Who can long deny the unrestrained love of a big-hearted long-legged one-hundred-pound wolf? Within minutes, Al was completely won over.

By the time they left, Al and Neil were in love with Shunka and wanted him for MacSkimming. They had only to convince David Coburn, Director of the school. As for David and me, we had been impressed with their attitude toward Shunka, the way they handled him, and the general philosophy of the school's outdoor education concept, which stressed understanding and respect toward the natural environment as a key to man's survival.

If everything was as good as it sounded, Shunka would have a good home—perhaps a better home than we had been able to provide for him. All that remained was for us to inspect the school, meet Coburn and, if everything checked out, complete the arrangements for Shunka's move.

Chapter 13

In early April the nights were still winter-cold, but the days radiated the warmth of spring. The maple sap flowed and buckets were hung to collect the precious, water-clear liquid for boiling into thick, sweet maple syrup. MacSkimming had a fine sugarbush, and David Coburn suggested we schedule our visit to coincide with the maple harvest. Leaving Shunka and Happy under Wendy's patient care, we headed toward Ottawa—and MacSkimming.

We left behind a muddy pen and yard, but the Coburn house still slept peacefully in a deep blanket of snow. A fire crackled in the living room, and David Coburn and his wife, Helen, spread a feast before us and introduced us to other staff members of the school. Coburn said little that night but listened to David's discourse on wolves—more impassioned than usual because Shunka would soon be lost to us. Whatever reservations he had about the animal, which I guessed were considerable, Coburn recognized Shunka's potential educational value to the school and wanted very much to have him.

The evening ended on a good omen. As we left the house, northern lights danced across the western sky in vivid greens and purples. I had never seen anything quite so breathtakingly beautiful.

MacSkimming boasted a complete 1890s pioneer village for the benefit of overnight classes and we spent the night in one of the square-timbered log cabins. I awoke to the heady smell of wood burning in a cast-iron stove. David had a good fire going and the cabin radiated warmth. By 9 A.M., Coburn was knocking at our door, carrying two pairs of snowshoes. We joined a morning class in collecting maple sap, and later with wooden spoons, scooped up hot syrup which, when thrown into the snow, crystallized into a delicious hard, brown candy.

That afternoon we were given an official tour of the school. The grounds encompassed 280 acres of bush, meadow, farmland, river shore, building sites and a rocketry range—each area designated as an open classroom according to the natural resources available. Every day, five or six classes ranging from grades one through six arrived at MacSkimming and spent the day putting into practice the lessons they had studied in books. Throughout the course of the year, every child within the Ottawa School District spent at least one day at MacSkimming.

We had heard of other outdoor schools, but none was quite so comprehensive or so impressive as MacSkimming. In a way, MacSkimming was the realization of one man's vision, and Coburn had fought hard for it—hustling to keep the school growing and expanding when there was no money, fighting red tape and bureaucracy to get what he needed. His philosophy of education was fundamental—"All organic life has a niche to fill," he explained. "Our purpose is to make the child realize that no matter how technical our state becomes, or how many buttons he pushes or switches he pulls, he is still an animal organism. He is chained to the land—whether he likes it or not."

There remained no doubt in our minds that MacSkimming was the right place for Shunka. Not only would he be well looked after and loved, but he would be an educational vehicle for thousands of children who, once coming into contact with him, might grow up liking wolves.

In our telephone conversation with Coburn we made one stipulation about giving Shunka to the school. He was to be provided with a four-legged companion, whether another dog or a wolf. Shunka had never been completely alone—excluding the one day Happy spent at the vet and during which time he had loudly mourned his loss—and we felt that the friendship of another animal was essential for his happiness.

We briefly considered giving up Happy along with the wolf so that they could remain together, but we knew it could not work. No matter how much Happy loved Shunka, her first allegiance was toward her master and mistress. To leave her at MacSkimming meant depriving her of any opportunity to fulfill her destiny as "man's best friend." She would be confined to the wolf pen and live out her days fighting with Shunka for the attention of anyone and everyone who came to visit. It all came back to the basic difference between dog and wolf. A dog is, essentially, a slave to man and looks to him for reward, punishment and survival. A wolf, however, generally prefers his own kind to satisfy his material wants and social needs.

No matter which way the stone was cast, we knew that one of the animals would suffer loneliness, and in the end we compromised—perhaps at Shunka's expense. The wolf was gregarious and easy-going, we reasoned. He and Happy had never mated and it was possible that in time, Shunka would form a strong attachment to another animal. Happy, however, might never recover from being abandoned to life in the wolf pen, and therefore it was decided that she would stay with us.

Sometimes arguments can be very self-serving. We understood all the reasons why Happy would be miserable living at MacSkimming—and yet we were quick to suggest that Coburn procure another dog to serve as Shunka's companion. We recommended he pick up a mongrel from the pound; an animal destined for the gas chamber would thus be given a new lease on life, even if it did mean confinement to a wolf pen. If that didn't work, we suggested that Coburn consider raising another puppy with Shunka. If an animal knew no other life, we rationalized, he could not be unhappy.

Coburn didn't have to resort to either of those methods. Somehow he had acquired a two-year-old female brush wolf from a local zoo. She was small and emaciated with a tattered, scraggly brown coat, but her eyes were beautiful and shone brightly with a desperate need for love. She was introduced to us as Sparky, and when we met her, she was still housed in the small chicken-wire cage which had been her home from the day she had been born. Many small town zoos are notorious for their maltreatment of animals. This one had been no exception, and Sparky was a sad example of such cruel and careless handling. According to Neil, had the school not taken her, Sparky was destined for an early death. The owner of the zoo preferred to shoot most of his animals at the end of the tourist season rather than spend any money feeding them throughout the slow, unprofitable winter months.

Neil, David and I crawled into the small cage with her, and Sparky became hysterical with pleasure and excitement, turning around and around in circles and yapping shrilly like a coyote. Like Shunka, she was affectionate by nature and loved people. Unlike Shunka, she was nervous, pathetically submissive and generally neurotic. She was so starved for love that she could not control her impulses. While greeting people with little wolf kisses, she nipped at ears and noses and in her excitement clung to clothing, her teeth accidentally catching the skin underneath. We were concerned that her "hyperness" and constant yapping would adversely affect Shunka, but there was also the possibility that Shunka's easy-going, relaxed dignity would calm the troubled little wolf. It was also possible that once the wolf pen was erected (it would have to be dismantled in Pickering and transported by truck to Ottawa), the open space would enable her to work off her excessive energy.

We returned home elated that Shunka would be going to a good home, and a little sad that we would be losing him. But that time still seemed far away. The ground in Pickering was thick with mud and would not support the equipment needed to dismantle the fence; the snow was just beginning to melt in Ottawa. It would be at least a month—maybe two—before conditions were right to make the move.

As the days grew warmer, Shunka began to lose his winter under-coat, the woolly fur falling out in huge clumps. The floor of the pen was covered with white fluffy balls, and the birds lined their nests with the soft down. We spent happy, carefree hours soaking up the sun on top of the shed, thawing ourselves out after the seemingly endless win-ter—pretending that those idyllic days would go on forever and, maybe, Coburn would forget to call.

Reality intruded abruptly on an early June morning when Coburn arrived at our house with a truck and three men. Work began imme-diately on dismantling the fence. We moved Happy and Shunka into the small pen, where they were to live until it was time to take Shunka to Ottawa. As I watched the fence come down, I felt a sadness which I knew would stay with me a long time. The decision to give up Shunka was now irreversible.

The fence posts had been sunk deep into the ground and were cemented in, which meant a fence-puller had to be rented to extract them. The large machine droned more loudly than a chain saw, and the noise terrified Shunka. He was already distressed at the fuss and commotion which he didn't understand—nor did he like being con-fined to the small pen.

As the machine started up its deafening roar, Shunka went ber-serk and, in a frantic attempt to escape the terrifying sound, he jumped up against the eight-foot fence—each leap bringing him closer to the top. Eventually, he would have cleared the distance, and I took him into the house, closing doors and windows against the noise. Shunka, however, was beyond reason and hurled his body at the panes of glass. I had never seen him so blind with fear. If ever a straitjacket was needed for a wolf, this was the time.

I pulled the curtains and held on to him as well as I could. Push-ing him over on his side, I forced his head down with my body and held his paws immobile. He lay on the floor like a trussed calf, but at least he lay quietly until my hands tired, and I was forced to relax my grip. Then the battle began again. David was outside giving Coburn a hand with the fence. I thought of calling him, but there was little he, or anyone else, could have done.

The fence was down by early evening and the world again silent, by which time Shunka and I were both so exhausted we had fallen asleep on the living room floor, my head resting against his flank. I felt closer to him that night than at any time during the year we had shared together. In two weeks he would be gone, and it suddenly seemed like a desperately short length of time.

The last weeks with Shunka were very much like the first—it was open house again as friends came to visit and spend time with the wolf they had met as a puppy and watched grow into adolescence. Every day was a farewell party, and I soon began to wish the day of departure would arrive so it would be over and done with.

One of Shunka's last visitors in Pickering was Mushka. He had not seen the matronly white German shepherd since Manor Road, when he had looked upon her as a substitute mother. He hadn't forgotten her, and as soon as she walked into the small pen, Shunka regressed into puppyhood and, bowing low before the dog, nipped and nibbled at her muzzle. But this time, their meeting took a different twist. Where Mushka had previously reacted with disdain and aggressive displeasure, growling and snapping at the eager wolf pup, she now humbly accepted his advances without so much as a bared fang. It was obvious that she no more enjoyed Shunka's attentions now than she had eleven months ago, but despite his ridiculous, pandering behavior, the wolf now towered above her, and she felt in no position to challenge him. Although her attitude was not one of active submission, it was submissive nevertheless—which made for a strange situation, since Shunka related to her as his superior. In this instance, the relationship ended in a definite standoff.

As the time for departure grew near, I worried constantly about the long, six-hour drive to the school. Knowing Shunka's hysterical fear of automobiles and the panic which traveling evoked in him, I was convinced he would suffer a heart attack before we got to Ottawa. We considered sedating him, but had read that high-strung animals—wolves

SHUNKA

specifically—could not be safely tranquilized. The line between the dosage that would calm him or kill him was so infinitesimal that the risk was not worth taking. Nevertheless, we consulted Dr. Reeve-Newson on the feasibility of giving Shunka something to relax him during the drive. He confirmed our fear that Shunka could conceivably die of fright en route. However, there was a solution. A drug had been developed which the forestry department used successfully on wild animals. It would in no way endanger Shunka's life. Since we could only guess at Shunka's weight, it was difficult to prescribe the exact dosage required to produce any affect on him. Therefore, Dr. Reeve-Newson suggested we try two pills a few days before the scheduled trip to determine their effectiveness.

One evening David slipped two pills into a piece of raw meat and gave it to Shunka. We settled on the back porch and waited—growing impatient and discouraged when, an hour later, the wolf showed no sign of drowsiness. Another half-hour passed, and in the middle of a wrestling match with Happy, Shunka fell over on his side and lay there blinking stupidly. He gathered himself back up on his feet and drunkenly stumbled around the small pen. "It seems to be working," David commented.

"I'm not sure. Why isn't he asleep?"

"Maybe it isn't supposed to put him to sleep. He certainly looks relaxed."

"Nothing is threatening him right now. What would happen if you put him in the car?"

"Let's find out," David said, and walking out of the pen, he backed the International to the gate. Shunka barely noticed the hulking green vehicle. David opened the back door of the station wagon and picking up the befuddled wolf, carried the limp body to the car and put him inside. Shunka still did not react. "Looks good so far. Ready for a drive?"

"Sure," I said, and shoving Happy in beside Shunka, jumped into the car.

If Shunka realized where he was, he gave no sign of it, but sat quietly, occasionally standing up and weaving around the back of the International.

David felt we should drive around for an hour or two to make sure the sedative had a lasting affect. It was almost dark and I suggested we go to the local drive-in, which would kill about three hours. Coincidentally, the attraction advertised on the marquee was a dog story, a tale about six Doberman pinschers turned bank robbers.

"How many, please?" the woman at the ticket window parroted mechanically.

"Two people, a dog, and a wolf."

She glanced into the car, shrugged and handed us our tickets.

We found an empty spot next to a young couple in a small sedan, and sat back to wait for the show to begin. Happy was having a great time, munching hot dogs, sampling pop corn and nibbling David's ears. Shunka propped himself on the single seat in the back and, resting his head out the window, sat staring intently with stoned eyes into the next car which was less than two feet away. Halfway through the movie, the sedan unobtrusively glided into another spot a few rows in front of us.

It was the strangest evening I'd ever spent at a drive-in. During intermission, the lot was overrun by dogs dragging owners toward the playground; a large percentage of them were Dobermans. I imagined speakers shoved against dogs' ears whenever one of the movie Dobermans barked—"Here, Rover. Listen, Fido. Can you understand what he's saying?" I doubted that "Rover" or "Fido" had any interest. Shunka and Happy certainly didn't and slept peacefully through the rest of the double bill. Shunka was still asleep when we arrived home a little after midnight. We knew the drugs would be good for at least four hours.

On the day we left for MacSkimming, Wendy came out to stay with Happy. We felt Happy had to stay behind. Shunka was beginning a new life, and he should in no way identify it with his old companion. Convinced that Happy would feel abandoned and distressed by Shunka's absence, we warned Wendy to prepare herself for a weekend of screaming and moping from Happy. As it turned out, Happy had a good weekend. Wendy was her captive audience, and the two of them took rides in the car and walks in the field. If Happy noticed that Shunka was missing, she didn't show it.

With the sedatives keeping Shunka dazed throughout most of the day, the drive to Ottawa was not as bad as I had feared. As a safety precaution, David had built a wire partition separating the front seat from the back of the car—just in case Shunka became hysterical while David was driving. It served its purpose. Fifty miles out of Ottawa, the drugs wore off and, suddenly realizing where he was, Shunka panicked. Although he had not slept during any part of the trip, he had been calm, occasionally resting his head on my lap. Now in his frenzy, he clawed at my head and shoulders and tried to squeeze his body between me and the side of the car. It was as if I ceased to exist for him in any context other than as an object which stood between him and freedom. He drooled and foamed at the mouth and banged himself against the wire screen. The last few miles seemed endless, but we arrived with a live wolf.

Shunka's pen had been set up on a hillside overlooking the Ottawa River. A thick clump of trees and bushes along one side of the fence afforded shade and seclusion, and a straw-filled lean-to built from square timber logs was his new shelter and lookout post. Sparky was already in the pen. Exhausted and still semidrugged, Shunka noticed her only long enough to give her a subdued wolf greeting and accept her submissive response before he wandered into the dense bush and flopped down to rest.

Sparky, however, was delirious with the excitement of people, open space and another wolf. She didn't know where to focus her attention and, prancing and mincing nervously, she moved from one person to another and a number of times haltingly approached Shunka. After resting for a little while, Shunka emerged and examined Sparky more carefully. It looked like love at first sight. At least they understood one another. Sparky's approach to him was both submissive and teasing and she followed him around the pen with her ears back and tail low and slightly wagging, repeatedly nipping his muzzle and whimpering softly.

Shunka's stance was completely the opposite. He felt comfortable in his new home and seemed to sense it was his domain. Perhaps the familiar fence from Pickering still carried his own scent markings and thereby reassured him—although that was pure conjecture on my part. Having missed the benefit of an adult male wolf to serve as his model, Shunka never learned to lift his leg as did other male members of his species. Instead, following Happy's example, he always squatted when relieving himself. Other than that small detail, Shunka instinctively carried himself in the manner of an alpha male. More reserved than he had been in Pickering, he trotted from person to person with tail held high and body proudly erect, granting each one a formal greeting. Only when he came to Al did he momentarily forget himself, and pushing his new friend to the ground, grabbed Al's cigar and rolled in it before downing it.

David and I watched the proceedings from a rock, where we sat and played with Sparky. I felt badly for the little wolf, but her yapping and nipping was irritating and I tried pushing her away. The more I repelled her advances, the more determined she became, doggedly grabbing the sleeve of my jacket or nipping me from behind. David tried holding her snout and calming her by clasping the hyper wolf tightly in his arms. It didn't work. As soon as she was released, she returned to her frenzied display of love. One thing we did not have to worry about—instead of her hyper behavior adversely affecting Shunka, he quickly took her to task for her poor manners. Each time she clamped her jaws around some part of our body—a painful experience since she lacked Shunka's jaw control—Shunka grabbed her by the ruff and pulled her away, gently shaking the derelict wolf. Sparky seemed to understand that she had done wrong and, for a few minutes, calmed down, meekly followed him around the pen—until she forgot and was again carried away by the madness which seemed to twist something inside her. Shunka was patient with her and, although he continued to reprimand her, he was never harsh.

We stayed in the pen for a few hours. Shunka seemed distant. He was worn and lethargic and spent most of his time underneath the trees or communing with Sparky. It was hard to accept that he was no longer our wolf.

Finally, it was time to go. Halfway down the hill toward the highway, we stopped the car and looked back. Shunka was standing on a rock in a near corner of the pen, quietly gazing in our direction.

"He'll be all right, won't he?" I softly whispered.

David nodded. "Sure," he said and started the car again.

A few miles later we stopped the International beside the highway and wept.

Chapter 14

The house looked tiny and the land around it naked without the imposing wolf pen. Nothing remained to mark its existence beyond a square of crumbling cement trench, worn patches of earth, and a sad-looking plywood shed which David knocked down the morning after our return from Ottawa. The small pen went a week later. Coburn sent a few men from the school to dig it up and it was erected at MacSkimming as an antechamber or holding pen leading to Shunka's home. With dozens of people entering his pen several times a day, a double gate system was a vital precaution against Shunka's getting loose.

As far as Happy was concerned, any anxiety we may have suffered about the possibility of her running away was needless. She wandered only twice—the first time, she was brought home by a little girl not much taller than the dog; the second time she was found across the road, herding seven horses into a corner of the corral. Both times, she was sternly reprimanded and, wanting so much to please, she never strayed again. The overall transformation in Happy's personality was remarkable. Where she had once been physically aggressive and irritatingly vocal in her demands for attention, she was now calm and unassuming—the most relaxed and obedient dog anyone could wish for. She no longer yapped, yelped or tugged on people's hair and beards and was quite content to spend hours lying like a rug at David's feet. The only indication she gave of missing Shunka was in her refusal to eat for a week after he was gone. Beyond that, it was as if, for her, the wolf had never existed.

The knowledge that Shunka was only a six-hour drive away and we could visit him whenever we had time made the separation easier. We anticipated seeing him often, but we didn't expect to be back at MacSkimming before the summer was out, nor did we suspect that our first visit back would be precipitated by a tragic event that still continues to baffle us.

Soon after Shunka had settled into life at MacSkimming, he lost Sparky. All efforts to calm the hyper little wolf had failed, and as the weeks passed, she became worse. Having been caged all her life, she couldn't adjust to the open space of the wolf pen and slunk around from corner to bush.

Her attitude toward people remained erratic, and when her teeth accidentally left a two-inch gash on the thigh of a sixteen-year-old boy who worked at the school, it became clear she would have to go. The little wolf meant well, but she was unpredictable, and as long as Sparky was in the wolf pen, Coburn could not risk letting students in to meet Shunka—which negated the basic reason for having him at MacSkimming. The accident involving the boy had been enough to bring the Health Department, the Forestry Department, the Provincial Police, parents' committees and the school board down on Coburn's head for keeping wolves and permitting them to interact with people. He had to smooth a lot of ruffled feathers and quiet many fears—and he had to give up Sparky. She was shipped to a conservation park in Colorado, and Shunka was left to mourn the loss of another friend.

Keeping his promise to provide Shunka with a companion, Coburn replaced Sparky with a young male collie from the pound. He put the dog inside the pen and watched for a couple of hours as he and Shunka ran and played. The collie was aggressive and showed no fear of the wolf, but there was nothing unusual in either animal's behavior and they seemed to get along. The next morning, the collie was dead.

When Coburn called to tell us what had happened, we could not accept it. Shunka had played with countless dogs without so much as baring his fangs. The wolf we had known was loving and affectionate. He was not a killer. It must have been an accident. Except that it wasn't, and as I listened to the story, I struggled against a growing sense of revulsion and alienation toward Shunka. I consoled myself with the inconsequential fact that the kill had been mercifully clean and quick— there were no signs of a fight or struggle; just the dead dog with his throat ripped open.

Bewildered and sick at heart, we returned to MacSkimming, not knowing if we would find the Shunka we had left behind less than two months ago or a deranged, bloodthirsty wolf. Our doubts and condemnations vanished the minute we saw him bouncing up and down at the gate, happy to see us and eager to greet us. Nothing had changed. He was as he had always been—boundlessly affectionate with eyes that still looked at you with open innocence. All was well in his world, and it was our problem to come to terms with what had happened. Remorse and guilt were human emotions; murder, a human crime.

Between moving and losing Happy, and then Sparky, Shunka had had to make difficult adjustments. I wondered if he related Sparky's disappearance to the collie—holding the dog somehow responsible for the loss of his new mate. David felt that explanation was unrealistically romantic—although not impossible. That Shunka killed the dog had to do with a complex set of natural laws of survival which we could only guess at. David recalled the incident with Sam, the street dog. Had Sam ignored Shunka's warning and continued to harass him, Shunka might have killed him. Perhaps like Sam, the collie gave him no peace—but, unlike Sam, he refused to give ground and show submission toward Shunka. In a natural state, a wolf who refuses to accept the established social hierarchy within a pack is ostracized, and he either joins another pack or becomes a lone wolf. Captivity creates an unnatural set of conditions and an uncooperative animal cannot leave or be chased away. Nevertheless, the status quo still must be maintained—even if it means killing the offending animal.

We could think up many reasons why it had happened, but we would never know. The only thing we knew was that Shunka was still the wolf we had raised and loved. Any doubts that may have lingered about his temperament were completely erased when we put Happy in the pen with him. When we first arrived, we didn't know what to expect and had left Happy with Helen at the Coburn farm. I suffered a momentary twinge of apprehension as the gate opened and Happy bounced in—but, again, the fault was mine. Shunka was delighted to see his old friend and after thoroughly sniffing, licking and embracing her in wolf-like fashion, the two of them fell into their old game of tag and wrestle. The only change in their relationship was that Happy had become more intolerant of Shunka and became quickly bored with his constant attention. She spent most of the visit with her little fangs bared, snapping and growling at Shunka or yelping like a spoiled baby when he playfully shook her ruff or tried to knock her down. He, on the other hand, did everything to please her—falling over on his back when she rammed him and allowing her to trounce him on every round.

We again considered leaving her at MacSkimming as a companion for Shunka, but it looked as if Happy would not stand for it. After a long discussion with Coburn, we agreed that under the circumstances Shunka would have to make it without a mate. Bringing in another dog could be asking for more trouble. Finding the right wolf would be difficult, if not impossible, since any animal living with Shunka would have to interact with people as easily as he did. And if such a wolf could be found, Coburn would be faced with the problem of a litter of wolf pups. He felt strongly that it would be irresponsible to bring more wolves into the world to be unnecessarily raised in captivity, and on that point we agreed wholeheartedly.

Although Shunka would be lonely for a while, he would not be alone. The daily visits from staff members—particularly from Neil and Al who both doted on the wolf—would help make up for the lack of a canine friend. There would also be daily visits from children, although for the first few months after Sparky's departure Coburn kept them out of the wolf pen, lining the kids up along the outside of the fence so Shunka could trot from one end to the other, kissing each face pressed close against the wire. From Coburn's point of view, he could do it no other way. David and I knew and trusted Shunka—but we were not responsible for the hundreds of students who passed through MacSkimming every day. Coburn had to be very sure of Shunka, and it wasn't until he himself had been completely won over by the wolf that he began letting classes inside the pen.

The following summer we had a wonderful opportunity to observe Shunka closely with children when we spent a week at MacSkimming filming an episode for CTV's weekly series *Target the Impossible*. We had been so impressed by the school that we felt it provided enough material for a strong half-hour documentary.

Shunka was again a star, and he was at his best with young children. It was amazing to watch a class of tough, streetwise ten-year-olds forget their studied attitudes of bored hostility as they happily ran and played with Shunka. Shunka loved kids. He played tag with them, let them scratch his head and rub his stomach, and freely gave out wolf kisses to eager laughing faces.

The wolf had become an important part of the school's curriculum, and visits to the pen were well-planned and organized.

Every class of ten to fifteen children was first taken into the holding pen where Coburn explained that although Shunka weighed at least 135 pounds and looked very big, he was friendly; that he liked to play, but he didn't like to be teased. And as each student entered the pen, he was told to kneel on the grass against the fence so Shunka could give him a kiss. Although Shunka could knock an adult off his feet by jumping on him unexpectedly, he sensed children were more fragile and instead of putting his over-sized paws on little shoulders, he substituted a gentle lick across the face for his traditional greeting. At two years of age, he was still a sociable and affectionate animal, but he had acquired an aloofness and reserve around most adults which completely disappeared when he was with children. They trusted him completely and loved him because he was soft and cuddly and furry. He sensed their vulnerable openness and returned that love freely, without fear or reservation.

He loved playing pranks, and he was still an expert thief. As the students settled into a circle on the floor of the pen to listen to Coburn talk about wolves and wildlife, Shunka moved in and out of the group, stealing a cap, sniffing pockets and, working carefully and delicately with his front incisors, untied a blue ribbon from a ponytail and ran away with it.

The *Target* show was a success and drew more response from viewers than had any other program in the series. Shunka was again in demand, and the following spring, David returned with camera and crew to film a segment for the *Friends of Man* television series. This time, however, from David's point of view, the filming was a catastrophe. The director wanted the same kind of free interaction between wolf and children that had taken place on the *Target* show, but he insisted that David follow Shunka with the camera on his shoulder instead of leaving it immobile on a tripod. "It won't work," David explained. "Shunka becomes submissive if I approach him too quickly, and I won't be able to get near him with a menacing looking object like a camera on my shoulder—he will be skittish and will skulk around with his tail between his legs." But this time David didn't have the same control he had had in the *Target* show, which he had directed himself. Consequently, he reluctantly followed Shunka around the pen with the camera on his shoulder. Shunka reacted as David had predicted and when it was over, David was almost in tears. Not only was the film he had shot of Shunka misrepresentative of the wolf's true spirit, but Shunka wanted nothing more to do with David.

After the crew left, David stayed in the pen and tried unsuccessfully to regain Shunka's confidence. David was not going to leave MacSkimming until the friendship had been reestablished. He stayed at the school overnight, sleeping in the pioneer village. At four in the morning, he trudged half a mile through the snow to the wolf pen. He sat alone with Shunka in the snow and shared with him the quiet intimacy of the night, finally beginning a soft howling which grew into a long lament. Shunka listened and whimpered—and then he answered, and the two of them howled together until there was nothing more to say except, "It's okay again."

Just before Christmas we unexpectedly heard from Coburn. He had resigned as Director at MacSkimming. He had been invited by the Squamish School District to open an outdoor education center in Pemberton, British Columbia, and he had accepted.

The question in everyone's mind was Shunka. Coburn wanted to take him to British Columbia, but the decision was up to us. We again drove to MacSkimming and weighed the possibilities with Coburn. Al and Neil were no longer at the school. The only member of the staff who had a strong attachment to Shunka was Coburn. Once he was gone, there was no way of knowing how Shunka would fare in Ottawa. On the other hand, if we shipped him to Pemberton, we might never see him again. Even though we had been separated for two and a half years, it would be like giving him away again.

Despite our attachment to Shunka, Coburn now knew him better and was closer to him than we could possibly be—and he had grown to love the wolf as dearly as we did. We knew with Coburn Shunka would be well cared for, and the decision was made to ship him to British Columbia as soon as Coburn was settled and a temporary pen erected.

The conference thus concluded, we headed to the wolf pen to visit our old friend. Several months had passed since we had last been at MacSkimming. Shunka greeted me as always, but he avoided David—remaining distant and aloof. It seems the relationship had never fully recovered after the unfortunate "fence" incident in Pickering and, as a result, Shunka's reaction to David was still evasive. We brought Happy in, hoping her presence would relax his guard. He played and cavorted with the dog, but beyond sneaking up behind David and sniffing his pockets from a safe distance, Shunka would not let David touch him. This was no way to say good-bye to your favorite wolf and in desperation—borrowing from a well-established lupine tradition—David marked a corner post of the pen with his scent. Shunka watched him and when David finished, he trotted over to the freshly watered spot, carefully sniffing—a puzzled expression on his face. David sat down in the snow and waited. His crazy scheme worked. It seemed to hit a familiar nerve in Shunka, and he turned and loped toward David, covering his face with wolf kisses and then throwing himself on his back for a belly rub.

We stayed with him as long as the cold weather would allow, and when we trudged back up the hill toward the pioneer village and a warm fire, we felt good about our decision. Shunka had had a good home at MacSkimming. He would do even better in Pemberton where, once spring came, they would build him a pen larger than he had now—complete with a trout stream. The new school was nestled in a lovely valley and the area was still wilderness. Wild wolves roamed the province, and Shunka might even meet some of them. Although he would be far from us, he would be closer to his birthplace; and we felt that, in a way, Shunka would be going home.

Chapter 15

Three weeks after Christmas, word came from Coburn. He was settled in British Columbia, the wolf pen was up, and everyone looked forward to Shunka's arrival—whenever we were ready to make the trip to MacSkimming and ship him out.

It was warm when we left Toronto, but as we progressed nearer and nearer to the Ottawa Valley, the snow drifts along the highway became deeper and the wind colder. Mile by mile, the brittle weeds disappeared deeper into snow, and by the time we reached the outskirts of Ottawa, the world was all in whiteness. We were cold. The heater in the Rover was pathetically ineffectual—no stronger than the warmth emitted from the embers of a dying fire. Wrapped in extra coats and buried beneath blankets, we arrived at the Coburn house late in the afternoon. Helen pulled into the driveway behind us, harassed and annoyed by her car, which had stalled and balked throughout the twenty mile drive from Ottawa. Nevertheless, she expressed delight at seeing us again and, still wearing her coat, put on the kettle and insisted we thaw our benumbed bodies before setting out for the wolf pen. We were reluctant to leave the warmth and comfort of Helen's kitchen, but our thoughts were with Shunka and we were anxious to see him.

As always, Shunka demonstrated unrepressed joy at our sudden appearance, bouncing up and down in front of the gate, dancing, prancing and talking to us in low, throaty rumbles. And, as always, the sight and smell of Happy evoked a response from Shunka that can only be described as pure rapture, as expressed by his frantic attempts to welcome his old friend with the ritualistic wolf greeting through the barrier of the fence. Shunka's consternation grew as we fumbled with numb fingers to release the padlock which had frozen shut and stubbornly held firm. The only way we were going to get into the pen was with the help of a blowtorch, and as David retreated back to the Rover, Shunka's disappointment at the aborted meeting was evident. He stopped his madcap dancing and spring-legged bouncing and silently watched David climb into the car, remaining motionless until the sound of the engine sent him into quick retreat from the dreaded vehicle.

I stayed behind with Happy, lest Shunka feel completely abandoned. I wished I could reassure the anxious wolf that we were not teasing him—it was not our choice to remain so tantalizingly out of reach beyond the chain link barrier—wanted to explain that David would soon return with the magic flame to release the lock.

I was stamping my feet and flapping my arms like a mad hen, having slowly grown stiff from cold, when I saw headlights inching slowly up the narrow, icy dirt road leading to the pen. A few minutes later the blowtorch was activated and the stubborn lock released. The gate was barely open before Happy shoved her way into the pen and the long-anticipated reunion with Shunka was consummated. The ritual was the same. Noses nuzzling and sniffing each other front and back—and then the final greeting as wolf and dog embraced each other, standing upright on their hind legs, front paws resting on each other's shoulders. It was like stealing back time, and for a little while the two and a half years that had passed since we moved Shunka to MacSkimming seemed to dissolve—all was as it had been before. Happy bowed teasingly low before the wolf and then dashed away down the length of the pen, the wolf following with a graceful easy lope, catching up to her, gently grasping her ruff within his jaws and letting go when she shrieked with feigned indignation. The playful love-game continued until Happy decided she had had enough of Shunka's elaborate attention, and satisfied that the friendship had been reestablished, Shunka turned to acknowledge fully our presence with the wolf greeting we were accustomed to and had come to expect.

As we watched him proudly trot toward us with the smooth, spring-like gait of a thoroughbred, his head high and tail relaxed and gently wagging, we thought that surely among wolves in the wilderness Shunka would have been a leader.

Despite his happiness at our reunion, Shunka was now a mature animal and—discounting the momentary relapse into unrestrained, puppy-like glee he had exhibited earlier at the gate—he now tempered his movements with the dignity befitting an adult wolf. Gently he licked our faces and, assuming a noble attitude, stood quietly so that we might scratch his head and rub his flanks. He stood as still as a statue, the only indication of his pleasure being the half-closed eyes and an occasional slow and sensual smacking of his mouth.

Despite a lifetime spent in captivity, he had developed into a self-assured and free-spirited wolf. Yet, despite the three, almost four, years of living with people—years of giving and receiving affection, playing with little people and big people, sharing song-fests—he never completely learned to trust them. His ancestors had been hunted, trapped and poisoned for two-thousand years, and this program of extermination has left an indelible mark on every wolf. Shunka was happy to see us, but I sensed a guardedness about him that had slowly developed as he grew into maturity.

The hour we spent with him that day made us intensely aware of his loneliness. Since Coburn had left for British Columbia a month earlier, Shunka had had few visitors. If we could have, we would have spent the night with him—but not having been blessed with a wolf's heavy coat and feeling frostbite creep into our extremities, we knew the time had come for us to go. Shunka's distress at our departure saddened us. He sensed that we were leaving as soon as we took a step toward the gate. He grabbed my pants leg—as he had done long ago in Pickering—and desperately tried to entice me into a game of tag. Had my feet not become so cold in the subzero weather that every step was painful, I would have gladly run and romped with him. Instead, I knelt down and put my arms around his neck, burying my face in the thick warmth of his ruff, again marveling at the smell of the wilderness about him—so unlike dog fur in that it really had no odor other than that of a cold winter night breathing warmth. David knelt beside me, and fumbling in his pockets, produced a crumbled, soggy doggy biscuit—a forgotten remnant from the old days. He placed it in his mouth, and as he had always done in the past, the wolf gently accepted the offering from David as a symbolic gesture of trust and friendship.

His most adamant stance against our departure was directed toward Happy. Three times he tried to force her away from the gate, hoping to stay her exit. But Happy's allegiance was with her human companions and, driven by the fear that she might once again lose her coveted position as family dog, she was the first one out the gate, pushing her way through before David had pried it completely open.

Despite Shunka's negative attitude toward automobiles, he remained in the corner of the pen closest to the car, occasionally jumping up against the fence and frantically pacing along the path he had worn through the snow. Not until David put the key in the ignition and the engine roared did he retreat to the far end of the compound. There he remained—front paws resting on a large rock, his gaze steadfastly fixed in our direction—and like a shadow he seemed to blend into the white snow and gray-black sky. "The great, white phantom wolf," I thought. And wanting to keep that memory of him, I didn't look back as we started down the narrow lane leading to the highway.

Helen had already made up the bed for us. We were exhausted but, dreading the morning and the ominous task awaiting us, neither of us slept. I stared at the sky through the large picture window facing our bed—staring into the shadows cast by a soft exterior light just beyond the window. Occasionally I drifted into a sleepless "sleep" of hallucination, always aware of David's uneven breathing and restless movement beside me, knowing that he too was counting the hours until morning.

And then the snow began—thick, heavy flakes made larger and more menacing as they streaked past the light outside the window. I closed my eyes, hoping that it was nothing more than flurries, hoping it would soon stop. An hour later, the flurries had developed into a storm and I watched helplessly at the swirling curtain of white which obliterated the sky and diffused the light into a distant, hazy glow.

"We'll never make it to the airport," I thought. "Dear God, please let it stop before morning." Getting Shunka into the kennel, into the Rover and to the airport before the flight took off was as much challenge as we needed. The snow storm, if it blocked the road, could throw everything.

All the arrangements had been made. Before leaving for the West Coast, Coburn had driven to the airline's head office in Montreal to arrange personally Shunka's flight to British Columbia—to ensure that the wolf would be carefully handled and well attended. He had also contacted Officer Rankin of the Royal Canadian Mounted Police and requested that a special dog handler meet the flight in Winnipeg to administer a second dosage of tranquilizers to Shunka. We had again consulted with Dr. Reeve-Newson about Shunka's sedation for the long trip across Canada and had got an adequate supply of the animal tranquilizer. Two and a half pills administered one hour before flight time should give us the desired results; and, with a booster pill administered during the stopover in Winnipeg, Shunka should sleep right through to Vancouver, remaining sedated until he arrived at his new home. Everything was figured to a hair's breadth, but we had not counted on snow.

The alarm went off at 4:30 A.M., and I heard David getting out of bed. It was time to feed Shunka the prescribed hamburger-encased pills. It seemed less than ten minutes had passed when I felt someone shaking my foot. "It's five o'clock," David said. "Get dressed. Kathy and Shoney will be waiting for us at the gate in half an hour. Helen is up—she's already made a pot of coffee."

I opened my eyes. It was still dark and the snow was still falling past the window, adding to the surrealism of the early morning and the task before us. I didn't think to switch on the light but dressed in darkness—as if the artificial light would intrude into my thoughts and break the spell. The hush of darkness seemed so natural to the moment.

David was tense and impatient to be on the move and worried about Kathy and Shoney waiting for us by the roadside. Because of the snow, it would be a strenuous drive for them from Montreal, where they had moved to a year ago. There are few friends you could ask to drive one hundred miles through a snow storm to help you move a wolf at 5:30 in the morning. But Shoney and Kathy were like that—they had offered to come as soon as David called them the night before; offered even before David could ask. I quickly gulped the coffee Helen had poured for me, barely noticing the hot liquid scalding my throat, thanked her and struggled into my winter cocoon. Neither David nor I spoke as we swept the snow off the Rover and headed toward the pen.

As we pulled onto the highway, we saw the headlights of a car standing in front of the gate which barred trespassers from Shunka's domain. Kathy and Shoney had arrived. Shoney climbed out of their car, and he and David discussed a plan of action. Kathy agreed to stay behind in their car with Happy—it would be difficult enough to load Shunka into the kennel without the dog's playful nipping and teasing. David, Shoney and I piled into the Rover and revved up the icy hill toward the pen, praying that we would find a sleepy, sedated wolf. My stomach turned into a tight knot as, approaching the pen, we glimpsed a white, furry figure pacing and bouncing along the fence which ran parallel to the road.

No one spoke and David's face was grim as he unloaded the kennel from the back of the Rover. It was a standard, large kennel such as those supplied by airlines to transport dogs. Comparing its relative size to Shunka, who suddenly seemed huge and excessively long-legged, the kennel appeared to me impossibly small and ridiculously fragile.

Shunka showed no sigh of drowsiness and, unaware of the purpose of our early morning visit, greeted us warmly and playfully. He was particularly delighted to see Shoney and beleaguered his beloved friend whom he had not seen for two months with elaborate rituals of welcome. David approached the wolf and knelt before him. Shunka licked his face and rolled over for the expected scratching of the stomach. Instead, David encircled the wolf in his arms and tried to pick him up. Immediately wary, with one quick movement Shunka bounded free. Now suspicious of David's motives, he carefully avoided him and turned his wolfish attention back to Shoney. Shoney hugged the wolf and lay down on the snow beside him, softly speaking to the animal through chattering teeth—presumably hoping to lull the wolf to sleep. I sat down behind Shunka and gently stroked his fur. He seemed peaceful and relaxed.

"Try to pick him up," I quietly told Shoney.

But Shunka quickly anticipated Shoney's action and again was on his feet and beyond our reach. However, having no previous grievances against Shoney, he quickly returned for more play and love.

"You've got to put the leash around his neck, Shoney," I said. "He trusts you. He might let you do it."

Shoney was nervous. His association with Shunka had always been playful and affectionate, and Shunka had accepted Shoney as a trusted friend and peer. Hesitatingly, Shoney took the choke chain from David. I knew what he was going through—that somehow it was unfair. Shunka had never had cause to mistrust Shoney's friendship and now Shoney was forced to betray that trust. The fact that there was no choice made it no easier. Shoney knelt and waited for Shunka to approach him. As the wolf pranced toward him and began licking his face, Shoney quickly slipped the noose around the wolf's neck and tightly held the chain.

"It's done," Shoney said, his voice shaky and full of unhappiness as he clung to the leash.

Shunka reacted immediately to the constriction around his neck and began to pull and struggle as Shoney tried to keep a hold on the wolf and rationalize his own ambivalent feelings. David quickly took the leash from him and the battle between man and wolf began.

Years had passed since Shunka last felt a leash around his neck, and it was now a foreign and threatening weapon. All his early training had been forgotten—training which he had never really accepted but had merely tolerated because it had provided a means for him to explore the world beyond his pen. He knew that we were not about to embark on a merry jaunt through the meadows—that what was happening now was somehow consequential. David tried pulling Shunka toward the open mouth of the kennel, but Shunka fought hard and forced the chain tighter around his throat.

We were losing time. We had to leave the school by 6:30 to make the 8 A.M. flight. It was now fifteen minutes past six. If we didn't get Shunka into the kennel in the next few minutes, we would not make it, and all the scheduling and planning would have to be started again from scratch. Worse than that, feeling betrayed and misled, Shunka might not let anyone near him to administer the necessary drugs.

I began to feel panic and fought against it. Panic at Shunka's agony, panic that we would not succeed—and panic that Shunka, who by now had worked himself into a terrifying frenzy, might in a moment of fear-crazed madness, kill one of us.

"Stop, David, let him go," I cried, as Shunka growled and snapped at the chain, grotesquely twisting his body in an effort to free himself. I had never seen him so provoked, never seen him bare his fangs with such unmistakable sincerity, his hackles raised, his eyes glazed.

Despite my pleas, and Shoney's hesitant suggestion that perhaps we should let Shunka rest a little, David held fast to the chain—Shunka all the while lunging and rearing, snapping his jaws and biting the chain. In spite of his terror and blind panic, he made no attempt to lunge at David or nip at his hands which were holding the chain. He must have known that if he snapped at those offending hands, his freedom would be guaranteed. From Shunka's point of view, this was a life-death struggle, but his teeth never touched David, nor did he direct his fury toward any of the people in the pen. I later felt my real betrayal of Shunka was that I had been frightened by him—I had, for a little while, lost faith in him.

Intermingled with fear was the apprehension that we would, in the end, kill Shunka. The story of another wolf kept flashing through my mind—a tame wolf who, like Shunka, had to be transported by kennel to a new destination. In the process of trying to force the animal into the kennel with a choke chain strung through the back of the cage—one man pulling the wolf and two men pushing from behind—the wolf arrived dead from internal bleeding, or, as the author wrote, "a broken heart." David knew the story well, and I knew that he too was afraid the same thing could happen with Shunka. But there was no time for talking and, not knowing what David had in mind, I begged that Shunka be freed—never mind the flight. David didn't hear me. Somehow he had managed to slide the wolf across the hard packed snow so that Shunka was suddenly facing the kennel, his head inside. Instinctively, I pushed from behind, shouting to Shoney for help. With David still firmly holding the chain, and Shoney and me blocking the exit, Shunka was forced into the cage and the wire door was snapped shut. It was only then I learned that instead of dragging and pulling the wolf inside by force of the choke chain, David had slowly inched the kennel toward the wolf with his feet.

For the first time, I was aware my hands were painfully frozen and, as I drew a deep breath, I was afraid my knees would give out from under me. Shunka skulked in the kennel, his tongue lolling, his sides panting and heaving. The choke chain was still bound tightly around his neck. Having been blessed, or cursed, with long, narrow hands, it was my job to remove the offending chain. With some reticence, I slipped my hands between the bars and reached toward the wolf's neck. The choke chain was tight, and I had trouble slipping my fingers between the collar and his neck. If Shunka was aware of my hands fumbling to loosen the chain, he gave no indication of it and continued his trancelike posture. Slowly, the chain loosened, and I slipped it off Shunka's neck, gently scratching the thick ruff and caressing his head, seeking a spark of recognition, some contact, but Shunka had withdrawn into his own nightmare and we had become a part of it.

The first stage of getting Shunka to the airport had been completed. The next step was to get him loaded into the Land Rover. We had borrowed a toboggan from one of the Coburn children and, hoisting wolf and kennel onto the plastic sheet, began pulling and shoving it toward the car. The scraping and bumping set Shunka into a new cycle of panic, and he bit and banged against the bars of the cage. David and Shoney had to use every ounce of strength to keep the kennel upright and on the plastic. The relatively short distance of forty feet from pen to car required ten minutes to traverse with our awkward cargo.

Every kennel comes equipped with a cardboard cover, and our vet suggested we try using it during the drive to the airport. Many animals seem to travel better if they can't see movement past the window. The cover was placed over the kennel, and Shunka and kennel were hoisted into the Rover. We could hear Shunka banging and pawing at the cardboard. The three of us climbed into the front of the Rover and, with Shunka still tearing at the cardboard, we began our slow descent toward the highway. I felt a sudden chill of terror as Shunka's nose nudged against the back of my head. Shoney, who had been sitting partially facing Shunka, suddenly paled.

"Good God, David, stop the car," Shoney yelled. "He's snapped he wires of the kennel."

The Rover skidded to a halt. Two corner wires had been bitten in half, and Shunka's gums were bleeding. The hole was not large, barely wide enough to allow Shunka to push his nose through, but the extra space gave his jaws better leverage to work on the rest of the wires.

"I'll fix it with some fencing wire when we get to the airport," David said and started the car downhill again.

"That kennel isn't going to hold him," I mumbled.

"What do you suggest I do?" David answered angrily.

"I don't know. Maybe we should give him another pill."

"With what? You have any hamburger in your purse? Or maybe a hot dog? Look at him—he's not going to accept anything from us in the state he's in. Anyway, I already gave him an extra pill this morning. One more might kill him."

"I'm sure he'll be all right," Shoney interceded. "He just needs time to get used to it."

By the time we arrived at the highway where Kathy waited with Happy, Shunka had shredded the remaining cardboard, but the rest of the wires remained intact. The bleeding from his mouth had stopped and although it was difficult to examine him closely, his injury appeared to be no more serious than a cut lip.

David and I were emotionally in bad shape, and our mutual anxiety fed on each other's. We each understood the other's pain and sorrow, but the understanding only increased the tension. In the interest of everyone's sanity, it was decided that Happy and I would ride with Kathy while Shoney accompanied David and Shunka in the Rover. At least it had stopped snowing, and the plows had carved a narrow pathway along the highway leading into Ottawa.

Kathy talked to me steadily and quietly as we followed the square blue vehicle which occasionally swayed and swerved as Shunka continued his assault against his prison. I don't remember what Kathy said to me, but her calm words slowly relaxed me. When David's hand finally signaled out the Rover window that everything was okay, I sat back—exhausted—and noticed for the first time that the sky had turned pink and pale blue, and we were almost in Ottawa.

By the time we arrived at the air freight terminal, we had passed from daybreak into early morning. Kathy and I jumped out of the car and ran to the Rover. Shunka blinked at us with sleepy eyes, calm and relaxed—looking the way he used to look in Pickering when David and I crawled into his shed for a wolf chat and caught him in the middle of a nap. The drugs had finally taken effect. We had forgotten that when we used the same prescription on him for the drive from Toronto to Ottawa it took at least two hours before Shunka was knocked out.

The rest was easy—paper work, forms, signatures. A brief moment of tension arose when the air freight manager informed us that Shunka might not make the flight—animals had to be loaded an hour before departure and it was now 7:30. David was furious.

Everything had been prearranged through the head office in Montreal, and they knew that Shunka was to be on that flight. Threats of reporting the manager's uncooperative behavior to his superiors proved useless, but telling him that if the wolf missed the scheduled flight and was left sitting in the freight terminal, he would within a couple of hours awaken from his tranquilized state and become violent seemed more effective. Pointing out the snapped bars on the kennel convinced the man that Shunka had to make his flight, and a special truck was commandeered to transport our cargo to the airplane. Although unauthorized personnel were not permitted beyond the freight building, David was quickly ushered into the truck and personally escorted Shunka onto the plane.

The drama was finally over. There was nothing left for us to do. Wearily, we stumbled into blinding daylight and found a coffee shop. Both David and I were physically and emotionally incapable of driving back to Toronto that day, particularly in the Land Rover, and we let Kathy persuade us to return with them to Montreal. We left a message for Coburn to call us there as soon as Shunka arrived.

The long-awaited call came a few minutes before midnight. Everything had gone as scheduled. Shunka was well and had arrived sleepy and relaxed. He had received his second dose of medication in Winnipeg and had accepted it without any problems. A reception committee had greeted him and, once securely deposited in his new home, he had graciously met the Trustees of the School Board and played with a group of children. Despite our exhaustion, the four of us in Montreal opened a bottle of champagne and celebrated Shunka's new beginning.

Throughout the following week, we impatiently awaited news of Shunka and his adjustment to the Coast Mountain Outdoor School. A letter from Coburn finally arrived, and we read and reread it. Shunka seemed quite content in his new home. He had made many friends. A little old lady down the road arrived each morning with hot buttered toast for the wolf, despite Coburn's diplomatic explanations that wolves fare better on more substantial feedings. Others brought bones and meat and carcasses. Classes of children visited him every day. He had made friends with the farm dogs and, as evidenced from prints in the snow each morning, was frequently visited by coyotes in the night much to the dissatisfaction and consternation of the dogs who viewed the wild creatures as invaders of their territory. So far, there were no signs of other wolves. Plans were in progress for a larger pen to be built when the snow melted and the ground thawed—a pen larger than Shunka had had in Ottawa, partially forested, with a brook running through it—a brook perhaps stocked with trout which Shunka could catch at his leisure. It sounded perfect—almost too good to be true.

Chapter 16

David was away filming in Europe when I first learned that the storybook happy ending was not to be. In early May a second letter arrived from Coburn—as troubled and troubling as the first letter had been happy. He wrote as follows:

From deep in the upper Pemberton Valley comes a situation report. I am well. Shunka is well. At the same time we are both unhappy.... The School Board here is enthusiastic about Shunka being a part of the school.... His reception, however, with the valley people was mixed. Mostly they were curious. They would come up by the droves on the weekends to peer through the chain link fence, mutter and turn and leave in their cars. Some people made a point of shaking a fist in my face. One was blunt enough to suggest that the only way Shunka would fit in this valley was to be "stuffed."

Then came the official response from Fish and Wildlife Branch. The Conservation Officer was in a most distressed state. His objections to the wolf were manyfold:

a) the wolf would stop the deer migration in the area;

b) the wolf would affect the moose movement and upset their feeding pattern;

c) the wolf's presence would attract in other wolves;

d) the presence of other wolves in the area would create a hazard to children;

e) the eventual escape of Shunka would play havoc in the valley.

We invited the Conservation Officer and his Supervisor to an open meeting where I showed the film [the *Target the Impossible* show David and I had shot for CTV], the slides, and explained the entire scope of Shunka's activity in the educational setting with children. I explained that almost 160,000 children through the MacSkimming School operation, had played, romped and learned from Shunka and that no child had ever been sent to the hospital.

The letter continued and included a copy of a letter to the school from the Fish and Wildlife Branch of British Columbia outlining the conditions under which Shunka would be permitted to remain in Pemberton. The wolf was to be enclosed within a double-fenced pen so that children could not reach out to touch him and it was to be "understood that at no time would physical contact be permitted between the animal and students of the school or members of the public." Coburn ended his letter by saying that "I don't really want Shunka to become a zoo animal here. In Shunka they have one of the most unique opportunities for educating children. They neither appreciate nor respect this fact!"

In reading the letter I was alternately sad and angry—and astounded at such blind ignorance, particularly on the part of the Fish and Wildlife people. I wondered at the motto on the bottom of their letterhead which read *"A Land Fit for Wildlife Is a Land Fit for People."* Apparently they have very little understanding of wildlife—at least of the ecology of the wolf. I had difficulty understanding how Shunka's presence would affect deer migrations or the habits of local moose. In a natural state wolves share their domain with these animals, and the presence of wolf packs in British Columbia has not sent the prey species south of the border where the wolf is extinct—which would be a natural deduction if one were to follow the logic as set out by the conservation officer.

If Shunka's presence did attract other wolves into the area, they would hardly present a hazard to anyone inasmuch as no sane wild wolf would go near a human being. The last charge—about Shunka's possible escape playing havoc in the valley—was the most ironic. The only havoc would be for Shunka and those who loved him.

There was an ominous note in the letter that troubled me beyond the inane comments of an ill-informed conservation official and, as soon as David returned from Europe and had spoken with Coburn, we began a tentative search for a new home for Shunka. Meanwhile, Coburn, Slim Foughberg, Chairman of the School Board, and Don Ross, Secretary Treasurer of the Board of School Trustees, were working hard to resolve the clash between the school and the Department of Wildlife. They were planning to bring the issue before the British Columbia Parliament.

On May sixteenth, Coburn forwarded a copy of a letter which Mr. Ross had sent to the Fish and Wildlife Regional Director requesting an opportunity to show the film on Shunka to further explain his educational value to the school. In the same letter, Mr. Ross pointed out that "there have been some remarks circulating around the Pemberton area attributed to the local Conservation Officer which are probably not in the best interests of your Branch or the Outdoor School with respect to the arctic wolf."

I began to feel more and more that the British Columbia Department of Fish and Wildlife might better be described as a hunting club than as a conservation authority.

On the morning of May 20, a Tuesday following a long holiday weekend, Shunka was discovered missing from his pen. A large piece of wood, normally fitted beneath the gate, had been moved aside and the wolf had evidently dug his way out.

A dead calf was placed inside the pen to lure him back, and classes arriving at the school spent their day quietly searching the bush for the elusive wolf. Because of geographical boundaries, it was thought unlikely that Shunka would have left the confines of the school property. The east end was bounded by the fast flowing, cold-water Lillooet River—and, given his fear of strange structures, Shunka would be afraid to cross the forestry bridge. A cliff dominated the other end of the property.

Just before noon, a logger stopped his truck at the school and told Klaus Fotsch, a staff member, that he and a couple of other loggers had noticed a large pool of blood on the forestry access road which traversed the school property. The area was immediately investigated—the blood was there as well as tufts of white fur similar to Shunka's. Fotsch took some of the hair and wove it together with fur from Shunka's pen. It matched perfectly, leaving little doubt that the fur by the roadside belonged to Shunka.

The fear that Shunka had met with disaster was compounded by a report by another staff member that he had heard two shots fired near the forest road on the evening before the discovery of Shunka's disappearance. He had been working near Ox Bow Lake on the school property when he heard the shots and looking up, noticed a late model International truck on the forestry road. He yelled at the retreating vehicle, and Klaus Fotsch followed the truck and noted the license plate number. However, at that time no one was yet aware that Shunka had escaped from his pen, and the shots were not related to Shunka's death until the next morning.

With the discovery of the blood and hair on the road, the pieces of the story began to fit together. A small marker consisting of stones piled one on top of another was placed over the site so that the heavy traffic from the logging trucks wouldn't obliterate the blood. On May 21, the International was again spotted on the forestry road. A man got out and destroyed the marker, his action increasing suspicions that the man in the truck might have killed the wolf. The School Board contacted Mr. Lawrence, the Conservation Officer, and requested that he investigate the matter.

SHUNKA

On Sunday, May 25, less than a week after Shunka's disappearance, the man who had been observed in the International truck was confronted by Lawrence and Fotsch and, after prolonged interrogation, admitted he had killed the wolf. Shunka's body was relinquished to Lawrence, who returned it to the school for identification and burial. According to his story, he had spotted a large white animal on the road. The animal had refused to move and, thinking it was a "crazy dog," he had shot it. In a later version as reported in a Squamish, B.C., paper, the man was quoted as saying he had "hit the animal with his vehicle and then destroyed it because it was severely injured."

Coburn waited until Shunka's death was fully confirmed before calling us. It was late at night when the telephone rang—David and I had been out celebrating our wedding anniversary and Shunka and Happy's fourth birthday. I sensed it was bad news when I saw David's face, and quickly picked up the extension. Somehow, I knew that Shunka was dead, felt it before Coburn put it into words. Quietly, we listened. It must have been as difficult for Coburn to relate the story as it was for us to hear it—he had shared three happy years with Shunka, and now we shared the pain.

For a moment, after the telephone conversation had ended, I felt a horrifying urge to laugh hysterically—except what I really wanted to do was scream my rage and anger at those responsible for Shunka's senseless death. Instead, I sat in silence, staring into space, not wanting to look into David's face because it was like looking into a mirror. We would never know exactly how Shunka died. We felt defeated with no place to direct our fury. Although Shunka died from a shot fired from a rifle held in the hands of one man, he had been killed by the ignorance and blind fear of all the people who had hated him because he was a wolf.

David finally broke the silence. "Shunka was right," he said. "He knew not to trust people, but we tried to teach him differently. We fooled him for a while—for a little while he believed us and trusted. Trusted when he should have run. Yet, inside, he always knew—and in the end he was right. It is man who is all screwed up."

"That which man cannot control, he destroys," David said. Perhaps. Certainly the wolf represents all that is wild and untamable—always a shadow lurking in the depths of the forest, his eerie, unearthly howl chilling the spine. Even in captivity, Shunka remained a spirit unto himself. He gave us his friendship, never his soul—that was always wild and free.

Thinking of Shunka, I remembered a book by Robert Franklin Leslie called *In the Shadow of a Rainbow*. It is the story of a young Indian's friendship with a wild she-wolf. Quoting an old Chimmayan Indian saying, Leslie wrote that "when anything strengthens a bond of friendship, the friends have walked in the shadow of a rainbow. When any living being is threatened with premature death, the Chimmayan believes that the individual has stumbled into the shadow of a spear." We had followed that shimmering, elusive rainbow with Shunka for a little while, but his time had come—and we lost to the darker shadow. Perhaps all beings live within its reach, but a wolf is *born* within the shadow of the spear.

The cry of a killdeer pierced the early morning silence, and as I drifted into sleep I remembered Shunka as we had seen him on our last happy night together—standing with front paws resting on the rock, outlined against the sky—the great, white "phantom" wolf. I hoped that in death he had gained the freedom which had always beckoned from beyond the ever-present chain links of a fence.